W9-BVO-466

DEMCO

THERE'S A SUCKER BORN
EVERY MINUTE

This Large Print Book carries the
Seal of Approval of N.A.V.H.

There's a Sucker Born Every Minute

A REVELATION OF AUDACIOUS FRAUDS, SCAMS, AND CONS — HOW TO SPOT THEM, HOW TO STOP THEM

Jeffrey Robinson

THORNDIKE PRESS

A part of Gale, Cengage Learning

GALE
CENGAGE Learning

Detroit • New York • San Francisco • New Haven, Conn • Waterville, Maine • London

GALE
CENGAGE Learning™

LIBRARY OF CONGRESS CATALOGING-IN-PUBLICATION DATA

Robinson, Jeffrey, 1945–
    There's a sucker born every minute : a revelation of audacious frauds, scams, and cons—how to spot them, how to stop them / by Jeffrey Robinson.
    p. cm.
    Originally published: New York : Perigee Book, 2010.
    ISBN-13: 978-1-4104-3653-5 (hardcover)
    ISBN-10: 1-4104-3653-5 (hardcover)
    1. Fraud. 2. Fraud—Prevention. 3. Swindlers and swindling. 4. Large print type books. I. Title.
    HV6691.R594 2011
    362.88—dc22   2010053993

Published in 2011 by arrangement with Perigee Books, a member of Penguin Group (USA) Inc.

Printed in the United States of America
1 2 3 4 5 6 7 15 14 13 12 11

*This book is dedicated to my friend
Special Agent Bob Levinson, FBI
(Retired)
missing in action*

CONTENTS

THE PATRON SAINT OF FRAUDSTERS

The patron saint of fraudsters has got to be P. T. Barnum, the circus impresario generally credited with the con man's motto "There's a sucker born every minute."

As the story goes, sometime around 1869, Barnum set out to buy the Cardiff Giant, a ten-foot hoax made out of gypsum and carved to look like a crude, ancient, fossilized man. It was supposedly discovered on a remote farm near Syracuse, New York, and, given the publicity that surrounded the discovery, was soon drawing paying crowds of three thousand gullible people a day.

Barnum, who knew a great scam when he saw one, offered a substantial sum to bring the Giant to New York City, where he felt he could sell ten times as many tickets. But one of the Giant's investors, David Hannum, didn't like Barnum's terms. So, Barnum did the next best thing and made a Cardiff Giant of his own.

Hannum is the one who supposedly said that anyone paying to see Barnum's copy proved the adage "There's a sucker born every minute." A lawsuit followed, during which the two men admitted that both their Giants were fake. And somewhere in the confusion, the quote by Hannum got attributed to Barnum.

Except there doesn't appear to be any record of Hannum ever saying it. Or Barnum, either.

Another story credits the quote to a Barnum rival, Philadelphia circus promoter Adam Forepaugh. He purportedly came up with it during an interview in which he tried to discredit Barnum by telling a reporter that it was Barnum who always preached there's a sucker born every minute.

Yet another account tags it to Michael Cassius McDonald, a saloon keeper and politician in Chicago during the 1860s. But his title to authorship appeared in a book published in 1940. By then, the expression had already been in print several times. In John Dos Passos's 1930 epic, *42nd Parallel,* it's attributed to Mark Twain, and it also appears in *A Yankee from the West,* an 1898 novel by someone called Opie Read.

The eminent amateur etymologist Barry Popik has since tracked half a dozen appearances of variations on the expression to as far back as 1857. He notes that early appearance in the *New York Herald* — "There is a new fool born every day" — and another in 1906, when the *New York Evening Mail* perpetuated the original myth by writing about a certain politician who will "get all the votes coming to a political Barnum whose motto is that of the original Barnum: 'A sucker is born every minute.' "

In fact, Popik's research suggests that the phrase was not coined, but rather part of an era, just one of those things often said by New York gamblers in the early 1880s.

A man frequently cited from those days was the notorious New York con man Joseph (Paper Collar Joe) Bessimer. According to a widely held version of the tale, Bessimer used the expression as an excuse to explain his criminal successes to the New York Police Department's Inspector Alexander (Clubber) Williams who, at the time, was in the process of arresting him. Williams is said to have repeated Paper Collar Joe's phrase to Joseph McCaddon, whose brother-in-law James Anthony Bailey was Barnum's business partner. McCaddon then took the liberty of re-quoting Bessimer in an unpublished autobiography.

The only problem is that Clubber Williams was a famously bent cop who couldn't be trusted to tell the truth, and there is no record whatsoever in the New York police or court archives of any con man — notorious or otherwise — named Paper Collar Joe Bessimer.

In the end, it seems that the origin of the quote has simply been lost to time.

But, the truth behind it, most definitely, lives on.

— JEFFREY ROBINSON,
NEW YORK

■ ■ ■ ■

PART ONE

■ ■ ■ ■

Chapter One:
A Two-Way Street Crime

Fraud is a very simple crime to understand — I tell you a lie, you give me money, that's fraud.

And it is never any more complicated than that.

Whether you're talking about someone who claims an extra $100 from his insurance company after a fender bender, a Nigerian government minister who is willing to share a just-discovered $40 million bounty with a perfect stranger, or scandals as big as Enron and Bernie Madoff, no matter how elaborate the scheme wrapped around the lie, no matter how complex the plot that a fraudster constructs to draw you into the lie, all frauds always boil down to just that — a lie.

Once upon a time, in a simpler, more gentle world, those lies revolved around wild-eyed, yet somehow believable schemes that made you healthier or wealthier. There were elixirs that could cure snakebite and also grow hair, guaranteed-you-cannot-lose investments on patents for perpetual motion machines, phony royal titles for sale, and miles of beachfront Florida property that just happened to be under a swamp.

In that simpler world, the caveat was born: If it's too good to be true, it ain't.

These days, more than ever, the warning still applies.

In our complex, globalized, high-tech world, fraudsters are more skilled in their craft than ever before, more elusive through their use of technology, more erudite in their understanding of human desires, and more sophisticated when it comes to pushing all the right buttons. In our complex, globalized, high-tech world, fraudsters have become the most creative and the most capable liars in the history of the universe.

Think of fraud as marketing, exactly like the advertising business. There is a product to sell, various tricks of the trade are used to entice you to buy, and once you buy, the "Mad Men" move on to the next customer.

This is not to suggest that advertising is a fraud. But Madison Avenue and con men use the same techniques to arrive at the same end — to convince us to part with our money.

Consider this: *Advertising* is everywhere because it is, essentially, ego-gratifying. We like being told we're unique, even if we are being asked to express that uniqueness by becoming part of a group. We are all looking for ways of fulfilling our dreams. We are open to solutions that will eliminate our problems and change our lives.

Now reread that paragraph and for the word *advertising* substitute the word *fraud.*

Consciously or not, we accept advertising because it offers us new ideas and, until now, the old ideas haven't always worked. Consciously or not, we recognize the fraudster's premise that a problem exists — a lack of money, a lack of status, not enough sex — and he's offering us a solution.

Academics suggest that the true power of Madison Avenue lies in the fact that so many people are fast to claim they cannot be influenced. They insist that they don't pay attention to ads, never watch them, tune them out, and that ads have no effect on them. These are the same people who walk around wearing Budweiser baseball caps and Fruit of the Loom T-shirts.

You hear similar things from people about fraud. I can't be seduced into giving some

17

stranger my money. I'm too smart. I'm not that stupid. These are the same people who buy into pyramid schemes — hey, if someone is going to send me $750, why not? — and order miracle overnight weight loss pills on the Internet.

Studies have shown that seven out of ten consumers believe companies use ads to exaggerate the benefits of their products. So if advertising lies to us and we know it, why do we still buy the products? Same question: If fraud is a lie, why do we fall for fraud?

The answer is because even people who are innately suspicious can be reached with the right technique. In many cases, that may not be anything more than flattery. You see that in advertising all the time. You're a rebel. You're a maverick. You understand that you're special, that you don't go where everybody else goes; so, be unique and join us.

It's like the scene from Monty Python's *Life of Brian* when the Messiah shouts to the crowd, "Don't follow me. Don't follow anyone. Think for yourselves. You are all individuals." And the crowd shouts back in unison, "We are all individuals."

That's advertising in a nutshell.

That's fraud in a nutshell.

Why did a savvy investor put his money into a gold mine that's buried under unreachable permafrost in northern Canada? "Because my friends wanted to get rich quick, and so did I."

In the business of advertising, and in the business of fraud, men are the easiest to fool. That's because inside every man there is a little boy screaming to get out, and inside that little boy there is a warrior trying to become a man. Advertisers play to that.

So do fraudsters.

Male sexuality and identity are wrapped around visions of a white charger, the rescue of a beautiful damsel, and living happily ever after. Because male fantasies are really little boys' fantasies, Madison Avenue knows it hardly pays to sell anything to the man when the one doing most of the buying is the little boy warrior. He's into winning and conquest, so Ralph Lauren and Rolex sell him polo. Not exactly the most popular sport in the world, but it offers strong images of a man alone, apart from the team, rugged, elite, and on horseback. That's also why Hilfiger sells him ice hockey — big, baggy team TOMMY shirts suitable for aggressive high-sticking, body checking, and slap shooting — and also yachting. The little boy warrior on the deck, alone against the gale-force elements. And that's why Nike ran their "winning is everything" campaign. They went straight to the little boy's warrior heart by saying out loud what so many little boys know but aren't supposed to say. "You don't win silver, you lose gold." And just so that no one could doubt Nike's intentions, an athlete added, "If I say I'm just thrilled to compete, blame my interpreter."

Polo, yachting, hockey, as boys become men, their toys become more expensive. They go from dungarees to $300 jeans, from Keds to $350 running shoes and then don't run in them. *Playboy* magazine used to put a one-page ad inside every issue selling itself under the heading "What Sort of a Man Reads Playboy?" A photo showed some dashing twenty-nine-year-old in a $3,000 suit, stepping out of a Learjet, with a knockout blonde carrying his crocodile attaché case, while he checked his gold Rolex Oyster before climbing into his Maserati.

When they're being honest with themselves, most men know that Miss October isn't going to show up just like that. But if the woman in the ad looked like his fourth-grade teacher — the spinster Miss Dribblenose with the horn-rimmed glasses and thick-ankle waddle — the boy warrior wouldn't waste the candle on shoeing his white charger. Instead, he tells himself, maybe, just maybe, some Miss October look-alike might say, "I'm yours if you buy this aftershave." So he saddles up.

It's the same reason he sends money to someone on the other end of an email addressed to "Congratulations Dear Friend," announcing his $800,000 second prize in a lottery that he never entered. Maybe, just maybe, this is going to make me into the dashing rich young warrior I'd really like to be.

Women can also be fooled, although not as easily. Women don't tend to buy sex. True, there is no shortage of con men playing sweetheart scams, looking for older women to whom they can promise love in exchange for expensive gifts, a place to live, a credit card, or access to her checking account. But generally speaking, women buy into security and expectation. Which is why the cosmetic companies spend so much money trying to romance them.

Back in the 1950s, manufacturers of lipstick, nail polish, creams, powders, soaps, and lotions realized that the woman who paid 25¢ for a bar of soap to get herself clean would just as willingly pay $2.50 for skin cream to make herself feel beautiful. The lesson was, women will buy into a promise. Charles Revson, the founder of Revlon, even said as much: "We sell hope." Today, that's the basis of the modern multibillion-dollar cosmetics trade.

It's the same in the multibillion-dollar fraud trade. Hope is the pitch. But this time the end product is deception.

Thanks in large part to the development of the Internet — particularly over the two decades from 1988 to 2008 when the dot-com boom came and went and slowly started to rise again — fraud reached worldwide epidemic levels. However, it was the economic downturn at the end of 2008 that put a match to the tinder, turning an epidemic into a crisis of pandemic proportions.

Suddenly, the planet filled with a huge supply of inspired offenders, an overflow of easily reached potential victims, and no sheriff in sight capable of keeping the peace. In the years since 9/11, law enforcement was detoured into focusing primarily on terrorism and illicit drugs, and fraud became America's largest single growth area of criminal enterprise.

So much so that over the next twelve months:

- Every man and woman in the United States — and, also, every child with an email address — will be targeted by professional fraudsters multiple times.
- One in nine American adults will lose money as a victim of fraud.
- Seven out of every eight frauds that take place will go unreported.
- Most fraudsters will get away with their crime.

Like advertising, fraud is a thriving multinational industry. But unlike the advertising business — or petroleum, telecommunications, and foreign exchange — estimating the size of the trade is almost impossible. Besides the fact that there is no public accounting, what numbers are published turn out to be little more than best guesses and vary wildly. Government agencies and crime watchdogs suggest that there will be anywhere from $2 billion to $100 billion worth of fraud in the United States this year.

Actually, it doesn't matter which figure you go with, or if you split the difference between top and bottom, because those numbers reflect only the actual amount of money that will be lost in the one out of eight reported frauds. Add in unreported fraud, then include the cost of repairing your life after you fall victim to fraud — the time, energy, and cash you have to shell out just to put your world back together — and the total skyrockets.

The tornado-like damage inflicted by a felony as common as, say, identity theft can ruin most middle-class families. If your credit card is cloned and used by someone else, you may find thousands of dollars charged to you. Sure, you can report this to your bank or credit card company, and, in many cases, the charges will be reversed. Under federal law, you're liable for no more than $50, and most credit card issuers will not oblige you to pay anything. However, if the phony charges are disputed, if the bank or credit card company suspects that you are trying to cheat — and they may not have any evidence to support their theory, just suspicions generated by an anonymous computer antifraud profiling program — or if you haven't put a system in place to protect yourself, or if you don't react quickly and efficiently enough, then it's easy to find yourself caught in a deadly chain reaction. Suddenly, your bank account is overdrawn, additional credit cards have been opened in your name running up further debts, and your Social Security number is being used by someone to apply for jobs and IRS tax refunds.

It doesn't matter that you've been robbed because the burden now falls squarely on you to prove that you're the victim, not the crook.

To set the record straight, you suffer the debilitating frustration of battling your way through hundreds of hours of phone calls, letters, form filings, not to mention visits to banks, insurance companies, mortgage companies, government agencies, lawyers, and law enforcement. While this is going on, your failure to pay the debts incurred in your name can land you in default. That opens the battle on a second front, with the risk of forced bankruptcy hanging over your head. Suddenly your mortgage, your savings, and the overall welfare of your family are in real jeopardy.

It is an all-too-common nightmare, faced by eight to ten million Americans each year.

Making matters worse, such is the nature of fraud that you don't have to be a direct victim to suffer the consequences. At one small company in the Midwest, a fraudster convinced some of the company's customers to pay out on false invoices. By the time the company discovered the crime, cash flow had dried up. Within months, the company was out of business. Forty people lost their jobs, and their families suffered the consequences.

There's no denying that the stakes are astronomically high. Yet, when you speak about crime to most people, it seems that our greatest fear is being attacked in the street or in our car or having someone break into our home. Understandably, we worry most about crimes of violence. Fraud is much lower on the list.

When you then mention fraud to people who have never been victims, what you often hear is, "I'm too smart to fall for it." Or "Why would a fraudster bother with me, I'm not rich enough?"

Like most disasters, until we're actually touched by one, we tend to believe these things only happen to someone else.

The problem is exasperated by film, television, and books, which often depict fraudsters as clever and charming Robin Hoods, handsome, well-spoken rogues who steal from the rich. We hand them cute nicknames, like Paper Collar Joe. And we romanticize them, like Grand Central Pete, who used to hang out at the famous train station to con people by pretending to be their long-lost friend from home. Or Victor Lustig, who sold the Eiffel Tower to scrap-iron merchants. Or George Parker, who sold the Brooklyn Bridge, Madison Square Garden, Grant's Tomb, and the Statue of Liberty to wealthy tourists. We turn "catch me if you can" Frank Abagnale into Leonardo DiCaprio.

Lost in the hype is that fraudsters are ruthless and incorrigible criminals who study, construct, and master crimes of deception; who unscrupulously target the defenseless; and who lack any conscience about the horrendous damage they inevitably cause. They don't commit their crimes because it's an amusing pastime or because they're looking for fifteen minutes of fame. They are players in a cutthroat business. They do it for the same reason that most criminals commit crimes — money.

Take a long list of criminal acts — murder, bank robbery, rape, extortion, car theft, burglary, assault, domestic violence, embezzlement, home invasion, tax evasion, drug trafficking, smuggling, fraudulent auto repairs, even pickpocketing — lift sex and crimes of passion out of it, and what you're left with are illegal acts carried out for profit. Like the famous thief Willie Sutton supposedly answered after being asked why he robbed banks, "Because that's where the money is."

If there is a difference between fraudsters and other types of criminals, it's down to the levels of violence that can occur. Not that fraudsters habitually avoid violence. The Nigerians, who have turned fraud into a national export, can be very violent. Every year, a handful of Americans who show up in Lagos trying to recoup their losses are murdered. But when two idiots in ski masks barge into a 7-Eleven with a sawed-off shotgun to demand cash from the till, they aren't interested in discussing the merits of canned beer versus bottled beer. They're interested only in robbing the place, using their weapon if they think they have to — or sometimes just because they want to — and getting the hell out of there fast.

Fraudsters are robbers, too, but their act is theft by stealth — where patience is a virtue — and they are more than happy to debate canned versus bottled if it helps them make the steal. The best of them understand that, when done in a calm, composed, and proper way, this is a low-risk, high-reward trade. That violence only ups the ante and greatly increases the odds of getting caught and then being punished. That the absence of violence puts the risk-to-reward ratio totally in their favor.

However, unlike armed robbers, who simply have to show up, fraudsters need to prepare the ground. Before anyone can hoodwink you into parting with your money, you have to be susceptible to being duped. So the con man does whatever he can to prime you.

That's because fraud is a two-way street crime. Somehow, somewhere along the line, you must be coaxed into participating.

Most of us would never open our front door and allow a stranger inside our home to steal the furniture. Yet every day, thousands of Americans allow total strangers into their life and then into their bank account. Most of us would never, knowingly and without force, hand our money to a criminal. So we allow ourselves to be convinced that we are investing, or cashing in a prize, or setting some wheels in motion to secure our family's future.

We become complicit in our own downfall.

To be a victim of fraud you have to open the front door. You have to invite the thief into your world, even if you believe that he's bringing you into his. You have to feel that, by giving him your money, you will somehow be better off. It's not just that you hear yourself say "I trust you," if he's really good, you assure yourself "He trusts me." You come to believe, against the odds, that the lie he's telling you is actually true.

After an armed robbery, victims feel violated but tend to think, "At least I wasn't hurt." After a scam, victims feel violated but invariably ask, "How could I have been so stupid?"

That's not an easy question to confront because the answer is both obvious and uncomfortable — common sense took the day off.

With that in mind, you and your family are at risk if:

- You have a bank account, credit card, checkbook, computer, email address, passport, driver's license, pension fund, gas bill, electricity bill, landline telephone, cell phone, fax machine, automobile registration, website, magazine subscription, personal stationery, business stationery.
- You are listed in the phone book, on the voter rolls, on a share register, on Facebook, on MySpace, or are on a charity's index of donors.
- You do online business with eBay, Pay-Pal, e-gold, Amazon, a bank, an insurance company, an airline, or any com-

pany that sells things.
- You put out the garbage at night.

This book is about keeping common sense on the job.

CHAPTER TWO:
FOOTPRINTS IN THE SAND
KNOWING WHAT TO LOOK FOR

In the early days of the twentieth century, a five-foot, two-inch seventeen-year-old left his native Parma, Italy, arriving in the New World, where he changed his name from Carlos to Charles. And while there isn't much to document his early years, by 1907, he'd turned up in Montreal, Canada, working as a clerk at the Banco Zarossi.

A small neighborhood bank that catered to recent Italian immigrants, it was owned by a bunko artist named Luigi Zarossi, whose trick was to bring in new customers by offering exceptionally high interest, usually double the going rate. However, because there was no way that Zarossi could earn enough through loans and investments to justify those rates, whenever clients wanted to take their money out, he could pay them only if he brought in money from newer clients. Smart enough to know that he couldn't rob Peter to pay Paul forever, as soon as Zarossi amassed enough of a fortune to keep him through old age, he scurried off to Mexico.

That's how Carlos, now Charles, Bianchi learned his trade. And as it happened, it was a trade very much in vogue.

From the end of the nineteenth century at least until World War I, a flurry of crooks repeatedly pulled that same stunt. Because banking and investing were largely unregulated, anyone who wanted to be a banker or investment broker merely had to set up shop. In 1894, for example, a New Yorker named Thomas H. Fisher advertised in newspapers across the country: "20% per month is what we are earning for our customers: can you do better?"

His ads boasted: "We frequently make from 100% to 300% on one operation. Why do we not keep all the profits ourselves? We are not clams. We are willing to divide with those who help us. You furnish your share of the capital and we do the work. We take 10% of the profits and you take 90%. Can you complain?"

When Wall Street officials did complain, Fisher's explanation was that he had nothing to do with this part of the business, that it was run by his advertising agent, Charles Lawton Work. But the authorities didn't care about Mr. Work; they suspended Fisher for six months, hoping that would be the end of that.

It wasn't. With Fisher suspended, Work moved to Philadelphia and set up the Investors Trust Company, which offered annual interest rates of 100% to 200%. He said he was able to do that because he dealt with stock manipulators and knew in advance which way share prices would go.

At the same time, a grifter from Louisiana named Louis Gourdain opened the Imperial National Bank in New York and ran an endless chain scam, promising to pay punters $3 for every $1 invested. He issued bonds for $1, each of which had four 25¢ coupons attached. You bought one, then sold the coupons to recoup your initial investment. In turn, everyone who purchased a 25¢ coupon was entitled to buy another $1 bond from Gourdain. So each bond generated $4 in sales to Gourdain, who promised to pay the original $1 bondholder the sum of $3. Eventually.

The bond was really just a chain letter, by which money goes to the top, while the deficit is spread out at the bottom. So while Gourdain made money, everybody below him in the chain had to keep selling coupons to make up for their losses.

Busted in 1899, Gourdain was hardly deterred. Typical of most fraudsters, he started up again, this time in Chicago, selling options on oil land. He and a partner bought ten thousand acres in Louisiana at $1.50 an acre. They divided the land into lots of twenty square feet, and offered $20 options per lot for 50¢. Each month, Gourdain sent his option holders a list with the latest bids for the oil land. Needless to say, the bids were always above the option price. Unsuspecting punters thought they were getting an inside deal and exercised their options. But there never was any oil, nor were there any genuine bids for the land. The $20 lots were really worth only a penny and a half.

Gourdain also got himself a seat on New York's Cotton Exchange — at least he had an office at the exchange and claimed to have a seat — using the name Charles H. White. He offered investors huge weekly interest rates for letting him handle their money. When the Feds came looking for Mr. White, he vanished back into the guise of Louis Gourdain.

Success breeds success and others followed. John G. Agnew opened the Washington Syndicate in Brooklyn, offering investors 10% per week. Nearby, William F.

Miller was doing the same, but on such a scale that he soon swamped Agnew's business and became known as "Mr. 520 Per Cent." Calling himself "The Franklin Syndicate — Bankers and Brokers — stocks, bonds, wheat, and cotton," Miller ran ads in nearly seven hundred newspapers across the country, promising: "We also Guarantee you against loss. There being Absolutely no risk of losing, as we depend Entirely on Inside Information." The ads cost him $32,000. But by then, he was pulling in as much as $100,000 a day.

Back in Montreal, Bianchi found himself needing money, so he forged a client's check, hoping that would take him to the United States. Instead, it took him to a Quebec jail for twenty months. Upon his release, Bianchi heard that he could earn money smuggling Italian immigrants into the United States. He signed on to that scheme, got arrested by the American authorities, and wound up doing two years in federal prison in Atlanta.

Now, at the end of World War I, and looking to start fresh, he changed his name again; this time he called himself Charles Ponsi — then altered the spelling to Ponzi — before turning up in Boston. He got married, failed in several businesses, and eventually started selling ads for a magazine that didn't yet exist. That's when someone in Spain wrote to ask for a copy of the magazine and enclosed an international postal reply coupon.

Still in existence today in around seventy countries, including the United States, these coupons are the global answer to a self-addressed, stamped envelope. Because the man in Spain couldn't buy American stamps to pay for the return letter from Boston, he purchased a coupon at his local post office, which Ponzi could then exchange at his local post office for enough stamps to send a response to Europe.

The coupons were priced at fixed rates of exchange, but from his years working in the Canadian bank, Ponzi knew that currency rates fluctuated. The man in Spain had paid the equivalent of 1¢ for the coupon, for which Ponzi's local post office was willing to hand him a 6¢ stamp.

These days we call it *arbitrage.*

"I wrote to parties in Italy, France, and Spain," he later explained, "enclosing a dollar in each letter and told them to buy as many coupons as they could . . . I reasoned it out that if five or ten or fifty coupons could be converted at a profit, millions could."

He didn't actually write to parties in Italy, France, and Spain, but on paper his calculations were right. So he opened the Securities and Exchange Company — long before the initials SEC meant anything else — and announced that he was buying coupons to exchange. Except he never bothered buying or exchanging anything. Instead, he simply invited the public to invest in his non-existent scheme.

By February 1920, he was promising 50% profits in forty-five days. Money came in. But when he changed the wording to 100% profit in ninety days, the floodgates opened. On good days, hundreds of thousands of dollars arrived at his SEC. By that summer, Ponzi had accumulated enough money to buy a twelve-room mansion — complete with such novelties of the day as air-conditioning and a heated swimming pool — and a controlling stake in the Hanover Trust Bank of Boston.

Exactly like Banco Zarossi, Ponzi's Hanover Trust catered to a growing Italian immigrant population and provided him with an air of respectability. Like the others who preceded him, Ponzi paid his first investors with money from those who followed.

What happened next was odd.

Toward the middle of 1920, a furniture dealer who'd sold chairs and tables to Ponzi complained that Ponzi's checks had bounced. It doesn't make a lot of sense, seeing as how he was running his own bank and, anyway, had enough cash coming in to pay his bills. What's more, the furniture dealer sued and lost. But once the claim was made against Ponzi, the authorities in Massachusetts began asking questions, and the *Boston Post* newspaper took a closer look.

In those days, a domestic letter cost 2¢ and an international letter, 6¢. The *Post* asked Clarence Barron, the financial analyst who published the still highly respected *Barron's* newspaper, to do the math. Barron calculated that for Ponzi to be covering all his investments he had to be dealing in 160 million reply coupons. But the U.S. Post Office reported that only 27,000 coupons were actually in circulation. So even if Ponzi had somehow cornered the worldwide issue of postal reply coupons for the previous six years, his profits would have been only $500,000.

The paper ran their story, and many investors demanded their money back. Ponzi responded, the way con men often do when faced with the truth, by trying to kill the messenger. He filed a $5 million claim against the newspaper and, in the next breath, announced a $100 million international investment syndicate. He concocted a fable about buying coupons in Italy, sending them to Holland, then on to Romania, Bulgaria, France, Spain, and Greece, where they were turned into local cash, then converted back into dollars at highly favorable rates. He said that because he purchased such vast quantities of coupons directly from foreign governments, and because those governments profited from those sales, he could not reveal any actual figures. But, he insisted, the money was there.

The *Post* responded with the headline, "0 + 0 − $."

In the face of adverse publicity, you'd imagine that the public might have pulled the plug. But Ponzi's explanation was so confusing, and his charm and guile so heartwarming, that the punters stayed with him. He personally greeted every new client with a handshake. And when the Old Colony Foreign Exchange Company opened up down the block, running the exact same scam, he pointed to them to encourage gullible investors — see, everybody's in on this so it has to be legit.

The Feds knew better and in August 1920 they raided Ponzi's offices. The Commonwealth of Massachusetts shut down Hanover Trust Bank, and a few days later, Ponzi was arrested. In little more than eight months, forty thousand investors had handed Ponzi $12 to $15 million. Many of them lost their life savings. His liabilities were put at $7 million. And, on the back of his bust, half a dozen banks crashed.

After serving several years in jail and being deported to his native Italy, he wound up dying in Brazil in 1948, penniless.

His legacy is the "Ponzi." And his ghost blithely lives on.

Today that ghost looks exactly like Bernard Madoff.

The life and times of the man who will go down as the most offensive, most repugnant, most vile fraudster ever — a man who defrauded charities! — was the stuff of headlines for more than a year. Just about every aspect of his thieving existence is now detailed in thousands of hours of television and a rain forest worth of books.

The short version of his bio reads like this:

Born in New York in 1938, he founded his own Wall Street firm, Bernard L. Madoff

Investment Securities, in 1960 when he was just twenty-two. Working his way up from penny stocks, he became the single largest market maker on the NASDAQ, which he helped create and where he once served as nonexecutive chairman. For a time, he was also the sixth-largest market maker on all of Wall Street. He had status and wealth. He owned homes in Manhattan, along the ocean in Montauk, Long Island, on Cap d'Antibes in the south of France, and in Palm Beach, Florida. He was a member of the exclusive Palm Beach Country Club, docked his fifty-five-foot fishing boat nearby, and owned a half share in a $25 million jet. He was on the board of several trade bodies and numerous charitable institutions.

Being visibly philanthropic is a favorite trick of fraudsters and a common trait among them. After all, how better to become a highly respected man than by demonstrating highly respected benevolence?

Madoff ran with the great and the good, was said to be worth $126 million, and had over decades consistently beaten the markets by producing above-average returns for his clients.

Socially just remote enough that his friendship was something to be sought after, tales abound of wealthy retirees in Florida

42

waiting in line for years to join the country club so that they could meet Madoff and wangle an invitation to invest with him. His friends got rich. And the rich got richer.

Then came the global economic crisis of 2008. By December, the financial tide had ebbed so far out that, if you weren't wearing a bathing suit, there was no place to hide. For Madoff, alone and naked on the deserted beach, the jig was up.

He confessed to his sons that his life was a gigantic lie. He admitted to them that, over the previous seventeen years, he hadn't made a single legitimate investment with his clients' money. That since 1991 he was simply spending their money as if it were his own. That the statements he sent to his thirteen thousand clients showing healthy returns on their investments were flat-out fiction. That after having concocted nearly two decades of deceit, he'd either stolen or lost everything. He was arrested the next day.

While it remains to be seen how much he, or others close to him, might have salted away, he is often credited with having lost $65 billion, although the SEC's estimate of actual losses is in the $10 to $17 billion range. The rest is accounted for by calculating the false returns he added to his clients' accounts.

In the end, his crime was a pair of simple lies to commit a simple theft, albeit on a gigantic scale. "I am trading" (he wasn't) and "Your money is making money" (he was stealing it).

That he pulled it off and got away with it for so long — longer than even he imagined he would — is absolutely staggering. But when you look at how he primed his victims to set up the lie, there are lessons to be learned. His story is a textbook case. And all the clues are there if you know what to look for.

What Madoff did was create fantasy, the same way advertisers sell designer shoes. He handed people the world they wanted to believe in. He gave them everything they needed to conclude that investing with him was more than an ordinary investment. That it was membership in an exclusive club. That it was a sign of status in a world where status matters. He worked the motto of advertisers selling *exclusive* — get the big snobs, and the little snobs will follow.

Had Ponzi not come first, we might today be calling his felony "a Madoff." But even calling it a Ponzi is a slight misreading, because you shouldn't think of a Ponzi only as a specific category of fraud. Robbing Peter to pay Paul is both fraud and the symptom of other frauds. It is the sleight of hand that con men use to keep victims from figuring out that they've been had.

It is the footprints in the sand.

Madoff's lie wasn't all that easy to spot at the time. Although there were some people who pointed fingers at him right from the beginning, and the SEC certainly should have figured it out. From 1992, they are known to have received six tip-offs, conducted three examinations, and actually went through the process of two full-scale investigations. Yet they never realized that he wasn't investing his clients' money, he was stealing it.

One reason no one cottoned on to him was because he already held the winning cards when he invited anyone to the table. His shining star on Wall Street. His successes. His wealth. His social status. His toys. His friendships with the great and the good. His high-visibility philanthropy. Bernie Madoff packaged himself so perfectly, it was almost as if no one would dare wonder out loud, Is he for real? He packaged himself so perfectly that no one thought to ask, At what point does Bernie Madoff become too good to be true?

Not that everyone who is packaged perfectly should be suspect. But every fraudster, almost without exception, consciously tries to hold the same cards that Madoff held. It's what fraudsters do. They seek the rock-star lifestyle, not just because it's glamorous but also because it's a spiderweb. It says: I'm rich. I'm famous. I have rich friends. We're all getting richer. We live in a tight social circle, and if I like you, I might invite you to join us.

Status rubbed off on anyone in Madoff's presence. But to be invited into the circle, you had to know someone who knew someone who knew Bernie. The reason he made it tough to get in is because once in, it's tough to get out. Again, the spiderweb. Once in, he knew, people would be slow to believe they could be scammed by one of their own. And, after begging your pals to help you get in, pulling out could put those friendships at risk.

Credibility by association is one of the fraudster's winning cards. He hangs out with famous people because that becomes a tacit endorsement of him. You hang out with him because that endorses you. It gets back to Madison Avenue. If you buy Armani underpants because you saw David Beckham wearing a pair on a billboard, you probably won't be able to put a soccer ball into the net from a corner, any more than you will be able to jump like Michael if you buy a pair of Air Jordans. Buying some actor's pasta sauce doesn't mean he cooked dinner for you, any more than handing your money over to someone — just because famous people have given him their money, too — means he's not going to steal it.

That's tough to see in the heat of the moment, especially from the inside. But it's not temporary blindness, it's irrational exuberance.

Madoff dubbed his investment strategy a "split strike conversion." Sounds pretty sexy, not to mention fairly obscure. According to him, it worked like this: He'd buy stocks of selected corporations listed as blue chip in the Standard & Poor's 100 Index; simultaneously, he'd buy put options below the current stock price to protect against large declines; then he'd sell call options above the current price to fund the purchase of put options.

Hearing that, it's easy to conclude, "I don't understand it, but he clearly knows what he's doing." The truth is, he never bothered doing anything of the kind. Yet, at the time, Madoff insisted that, given the right market conditions, this method ensured his investors steady returns of over

10% per year, whether the market went up or down. And a lot of folks figured, sounds good to me.

Not in the least convinced, in May 2001, *Barron's* newspaper posed a serious question: How could Madoff achieve such remarkably steady returns when so many others duplicating his strategy couldn't even come close?

Knowledgeable people on the fringe of this agreed, but Madoff had much of the world snowed with his perfectly packaged image. Eight years after the *Barron's* article, the New York State indictment against Madoff outlined a bunch of footprints — they used the term *red flags* — that should have been spotted.

- **Strategy? What Strategy?** There's an old adage that goes, If an investment adviser cannot explain his strategy in one sentence so that his grandmother can understand it, be suspicious. Split strike conversion? Madoff managed to get otherwise knowledgeable investors to suspend their belief in old adages. Even then, questioned about anything, Madoff's answers were notably vague. For example, asked about allocating profits among investors, he answered,

48

"It works out in the end."

- **The Lesson:** If you don't understand what someone is doing with your money, don't let him do it.

- **Tell Me Again About His Track Record.** Madoff never promised spectacular gains because he was smart enough to know that serious players are innately suspicious of spectacular gains. Instead, he offered healthy but not outrageous returns in the 12% to 14% range. He consistently beat the market. Except he was too consistent. Double-digit gains are great when the market is good, but when the market turns, then what?

  - **The Lesson:** It's a virtual impossibility to beat the market month after month and year after year. Anyone who says he's doing it, or can do it, is delusional or lying.

- **Why Not Take the Money?** Bizarrely, Madoff didn't charge fees for his money management services. He said his only compensation came from the commissions he would have otherwise been paid had his clients directed trading themselves. He told *Barron's,* "We're perfectly happy to just earn commissions on the trades." But when you take into account the supposed size of the Madoff operation, why would he turn his back on commissions worth $200 to $300 million a year?

- **The Lesson:** Shades of fraudsters past — "Why do we not keep all the profits ourselves? We are not clams."

- **Anyone Seen the Accountants?** Madoff was a big hitter so you'd expect him to be using a big hitter's accounting firm to conduct audits and verify his accounts. Instead, he used an unknown operation forty-five minutes away in a New Jersey strip mall. Three people sharing a thirteen-by-eighteen-foot office — one accountant, one secretary, and one seventy-eight-year-old who, it seemed, lived in Florida.
  - **The Lesson:** Real big businesses have real big accountants who do real big audits.

- **Why Use a Calendar?** Madoff

claimed that he pulled out of the market at the end of each quarter and put the funds into Treasury Bills. But investment opportunities span the end of one quarter and the beginning of another. There is absolutely no reason why any strategy involves closing out at the end of the quarter — except to reduce transparency. His end-of-the-quarter dupe was an "I've got a better idea" lie to hide the fact that he wasn't trading.

- **The Lesson:** When someone is out of step with the rest of the world, don't automatically buy into his rationale that the rest of the world is out of step with him.

- **Whatever Happened to All That High Tech?** Madoff's firm pioneered electronic trading in the 1970s and always had a reputation for being way ahead of the curve. Yet his investors did not have electronic access to their accounts. Madoff reported their trades several days after the fact and always on paper via snail mail. It's now obvious he did that to buy the time he needed to produce fictitious trade tickets. Someone should have noticed.

- **The Lesson:** When the man holding your money doesn't deliver on the hype he used to get your money, you need to ask why.

- **Hands-on to Keep the Secret.** It's one thing if a great chef has a secret recipe, charges you a lot of money to prepare the dish, and you love it. It's another thing if an investment manager has a secret to his success that is so closely guarded no one can figure it out or even have a quick peek. Given enough time, any great chef can work out the secret recipe of another great chef. Given enough time, any investment manager should be suspicious of another's methods if he can't. It is not surprising that, with secrets to protect, Madoff was a control freak. He made certain that his employees, his clients, and the regulators knew as little as possible. It is understandable that when you're in the midst of stealing and losing $65 billion, unless you keep all the holes tightly plugged, the secret is going to leak out.
  - **The Lesson:** Beware of people answering questions with ex-

cuses, such as: "It's proprietary" and "It's much too complicated to explain right now" and "If everybody else knew, then everybody else could do it." Control freaks guarding secrets have something to hide. Transparency and straightforward answers really do matter.

Whether it's $65 billion or $6,500, all fraudsters leave footprints in the sand. You'll spot them if you take the time to look. And when you do spot them, even if others are saying it can't be true, believe what you see with your own eyes.

CHAPTER THREE:
GREED AND BENEVOLENCE

What motivates someone to get involved in a scheme that seems too good to be true? Try the most quoted line from the film *Wall Street,* when Gordon Gekko proclaims, "Greed is good."

Everyone loves to get something for nothing. We'd all like to get rich quick. Each of us, in our own way, is waiting for our ship to come in with a once-in-a-lifetime, really terrific, unique opportunity that will change our lives forever.

At some time or other, we all believe in the Tooth Fairy.

Which is why money-for-free is big business. The con man dangles the prize a fingertip out of reach — almost just close enough to grab — knowing that when greed takes over, it generates careless excitement and that leads to stupidity. How else can you explain anyone falling for this story?

It's a bailout. The government of Japan,

realizing that its largest commercial banks are about to go bankrupt, has put together a pool of fifteen major international banks — so-called prime banks — to rescue the economy. Through them, Japan is offering $12 billion worth of financial instruments, in $10 million tranches, with a guaranteed 12.5% interest per month.

Not per year. Per *month!*

However, while the Japanese stand firmly behind the debt, there are two important restrictions legally placed on every participating bank. First, no bank can sell any of these instruments to an entity other than a foreign government or another prime bank. And, second, because the Japanese economy is so fragile, no government or bank involved in this can ever admit publicly that these financial instruments exist.

With that in mind, a man who says that he wants to become your new best friend explains that he has miraculously tapped into this lucrative market and obtained one of these ultrahigh-interest notes. Because the average investor cannot possibly pay $10 million, he has subdivided his into $100,000 parcels. After the prime banks take their 2.5%, and he takes his mere 1% commission — there it is again, "Why do we not keep all the profits ourselves? We are not clams." — he's inviting you to reap 9% per month, or $9,000 a month for each $100,000 you invest.

Frankly, anyone with half a brain should instantly question 9% monthly interest. A loan from the Mafia earns the mob only one point a week, or 4% per month. But greed can exterminate common sense.

You must remember, comes the caveat from the con man, the secrecy clause forbids governments and banks from acknowledging the existence of this unique and exclusive investment opportunity. Even if they were allowed to tell you about it, they wouldn't because they don't want you in on it. Governments and the prime banks have conspired to keep it for themselves.

You are warned: If you phone a government agency or one of the prime banks to ask about it, they will go blue in the face telling you it's not for real. They will probably try to frighten you away by saying it's nothing more than a con. So you phone a few banks to ask about this ultrahigh-yield investment, and they all assure you it doesn't exist. Hah, you conclude, if the banks are covering it up, obviously, it must exist.

THE BOY ON WATER BUFFALO RUBY

It does exist. That's what Gilbert Allen Ziegler wanted his victims to believe.

Born in Seattle in 1951, the heavyset, balding Ziegler claimed that he was a university graduate, but never coughed up the name of the school. He claimed that in the 1970s he was the president of a business college, but never named that school, either. He claimed to be an ordained minister, and though he admitted he didn't have any formal training, he dodged the specifics of who ordained him. He said he had a masters of business and a doctorate, but never said from where.

Armed with this made-up identity, he arrived on the Caribbean island of Grenada carrying a piece of paper that said he was chairman of the First International Bank (FIB), licensed in the Pacific jurisdiction of Nauru. (Ziegler invented a bogus bank that sounded like a real one — in confusion there is profit — but had no relationship with anything legitimate.)

Suspicious yet?

Clearly, the Grenadians weren't. At the time, they were looking to expand their offshore banking sector. He promised to bring wealth to the island, if they would grant him the right to fold FIB into a new entity, the First International Bank of Grenada (FIBG). The locals were happy to say yes but did insist that he had to capitalize FIBG with $2.2 million. He didn't have it, so he produced documentation for a ten-thousand-karat ruby called "Boy on Water Buffalo." He claimed it was worth $20 million but was willing to list it on FIBG's books as the main asset behind the bank, with the "fire sale" value of $15 million.

Legitimate banks are not backed by a single ruby. But that became moot because Ziegler didn't own it, didn't have any rights to it, and, in fact, never even saw it. All he had was a photocopy of an appraisal for the ruby.

Not the actual appraisal — which was totally suspect, anyway — but a *photocopy* of it!

And based on nothing more than that, the government of Grenada granted FIBG a license to be a Class I Offshore Bank.

Ziegler then bought a passport from Grenada, which the authorities there issued to him under a newly assumed name. He decided to call himself Van Arthur Brink, and they obliged.

Next, he set up the International Deposit (re)Insurance Corporation on the island of Nevis. Known as IDIC, the name was deliberately similar to America's Federal Deposit Insurance Corporation (FDIC), inferring a relationship and/or suggesting that this was even better because it was the international version. Once that was in place, he announced that the IDIC had awarded FIBG its highest AAA rating and, based on that rating, would insure all of FIBG's deposits. Needless to say, the rating and the insurance were as worthless as the photocopy of the ruby's value, because Ziegler/Brink had simply made them up.

With FIBG and the IDIC in place, he began constructing a network of franchised sales agents who, in turn, set up subbanks of FIBG, many of them also chartered in Grenada. His idea was that the subbanks created a conduit for income derived from the frauds that would flow into FIBG, where the proceeds would be disguised as legitimate accounts. Most of FIBG's nearly two dozen subbanks were run by alleged fraudsters, previously convicted fraudsters, or since convicted fraudsters.

Ziegler/Brink also took a valuable lesson from Las Vegas. Casinos invite gamblers on all-expenses-paid junkets just to have a shot at their bankroll, so he invited potential victims to Grenada to have a shot at theirs. He put them up at a good hotel, wined and dined them, dazzled them with white sand beaches and scuba diving, confirmed their worst fears about oppressive U.S. and Canadian tax regimes, set up accounts for them, and helped himself to their money.

If there is such a thing as a free lunch, this wasn't it.

He pledged to his clients that, on top of IDIC's guarantee of their funds, for every dollar FIBG held on deposit, the bank maintained $200 worth of cash, cash equivalent instruments, and gold at various international banks — including gold bullion certificates of deposit (CDs) from Union Bank of Switzerland. Never mind that UBS did not issue gold bullion CDs, he had documentation for the gold in the form of more photocopies of photocopies.

He bragged, "I know of no other bank in the world which operates with First Bank's underlying financial strength in support of its obligations to depositors."

Sadly, he was wrong. The world is filled with offshore banks whose underlying support of its obligations to depositors are just as fraudulent as his.

For every website on the Internet warning the public about superhigh-yield investments, including prime bank fraud . . .

- Offshore Alert (www.offshorebusiness
  .com)
- U.S. Securities and Exchange Commission (www.sec.gov/divisions/
  enforce/primebank.shtml)
- Office of the Comptroller of the Currency (www.occ.treas.gov/AntiFraud
  Consumer.htm)

. . . there are literally thousands of sites offering investors the opportunity to lose their money with high-yield investment programs. Scammers deal in hot air, couched in ambiguous terms to confuse investors, such as Prime Bank Notes, U.S. Federal Banking Programs, Discounted Bank Guarantees, Limited Edition De-Facto Treasury Securities, Mid-Term Notes, standby letters of credit, callable conditional sight drafts, and negotiable but irrevocable clear SWIFT wire transfers. Or they deal in the totally bizarre world of Federal Reserve Notes recently discovered some seventy years after a World War II transport plane crashed in the Philippines; Hawaiian dollars, bills stamped with the word *Hawaii* in the wake of the 1941 attack on Pearl Harbor just in case the Japanese landed and tried to spend whatever they looted; Railway Bonds; Czarist Russia Bonds; or Nazi German

Gold Bearer Shares.

Whatever the investment vehicle that's put on the table, it's fiction playing off greed. The deals are shrouded in secrecy and vagaries to conceal the commercial basis for such phenomenal returns. But the footprints of fraud are always evident, often acting like flashing neon warning signs:

- Spectacular returns
- Exclusive investment leverage
- Unique opportunity available only to the chosen few
- Little or no risk
- Highly secretive
- Guaranteed by the top 100 world banks

One group in Pennsylvania recently got busted for stealing $13 million from five victims after offering returns up to 140% weekly. Typically, it was "absolutely confidential" and available to ultra-wealthy investors by invitation only. If you were one of the chosen few, time was of the essence and "ultimate discretion" was essential. Naturally, there were plenty of guarantees that the program was completely safe: "Funds are held in a nondepletion attorney account"; "Investors' funds are only used as collateral for the transactions"; "Transactional risk has been eliminated."

Good yield is one thing. Idiotically high yield is impossible.

Put another way: There is, categorically, no legitimate investment or banking instrument in existence that can possibly generate weekly returns of up to 140%! None. Zero. Nada. Zilch. It's fraud!

If you don't believe that, it is only because you don't want to believe that. It is astonishing how many people getting involved with scams like prime bank fraud can look you straight in the eye and insist, "You're just saying it's a scam because the government doesn't want private citizens to make this much money." Or, "There's a conspiracy between the government and the big banks to keep little guys out of this."

Marketing primarily to members of evangelical churches in the United States and Canada, Ziegler/Brink handed out big portions of religious kinship to undermine their natural skepticism toward strangers asking for money. Sometimes categorized as "affinity fraud," he gained their trust by reminding them of all the affinities they shared, of all the things they had in common, and that he was an ordained minister. He assured pensioners on fixed incomes that, together with God, he could alleviate their worries about money. He targeted people who could least afford to lose their life's savings and least afford to fight back, shamelessly playing off their financial insecurities and religious beliefs: "God means for everyone to have the kind of freedom that comes with wealth."

Some six thousand members of evangelical churches, pensioners, and others handed him more than $200 million.

He worked the scam for a couple of years, until too many questions were being asked, then helped himself to whatever he could grab — several million dollars — and headed for, of all places, Uganda. He found a teenage hooker at the bar of the Sheraton Hotel in Kampala and married her, because being married to a local meant the government couldn't extradite him.

And that might have been the end of that, except it hardly ever is when fraudsters are concerned. Exposed for the thieves that they are, many run a second scam off the back of the first. As long as there are enough defrauded investors clamoring to get their money back, it's not unusual to see them pop up with an investors' reclamation group.

True to form, Ziegler/Brink reinvented himself yet again, this time as Ira M. Samuels, a fellow investor who'd lost money. He hit online bulletin boards, chat rooms, and forums, explaining that he was organizing a team of private detectives, lawyers, bankers, accountants, butchers, bakers, and candlestick makers to get everyone's money back. He claimed he was doing this for the common good of the human race and that he already had his team in place, ready to pounce. Then, he added, if like-minded defrauded investors want to share the booty, all they have to do is send money.

A few did. And there he sat running this new scam, until the Feds indicted him and the U.S. marshals struck a deal with the Uganda National Police. They raided his villa, dragged him in chains onto a plane, and amid screams of "You can't kidnap me," they kidnapped him. He died in prison a couple of years later. But not before he ruined the lives of six thousand people — and their families — who bought into his lie that 9% interest per month is real.

What they probably knew but failed to accept was that investment returns are a factor of risk.

This equation is irrefutable: Low risk

equals low returns; high risk equals high returns.

Your Best Defense

You protect yourself from thieves like Ziegler/Brink simply by turning that equation around: High returns equal high risk.

Before handing over your money to anyone, you need to look carefully at those risks. Legitimate investment brokers are required by law to spell out risks. Con men are required by professional temperament to downplay them or claim they are nonexistent.

The following statements are irrefutable:

- If the return is very high and someone downplays the risk, something's wrong.
- If there is an element of rush — you've got to get in on this right now — stay out until you can get professional advice and properly assess it.
- If there is an element of secrecy — we can't tell you because if everyone knew, this wouldn't work — you should assume it won't work.
- Successful entrepreneurs, who will tell you they are not risk takers but rather risk minimizers, always say that when they go into a deal, they don't worry

66

about how much they will make — because that's something they can often control — they worry most about how much they can lose if it goes wrong. Don't allow anyone to blind you with potentially huge profits; worry instead about the possibility of losses. *Downside* is what really matters.

IN THE NAME OF GOD

Ziegler/Brink's play to religion is standard operating procedure and happens more frequently than most people realize.

Fraudsters misuse the word of God to create confusion. Faith in Him is confidence in me, and confidence in me is faith in Him. And in confusion there is profit.

The Bible says: "Blessed is he that considereth the poor." The fraudster preaches: I can help you feel truly blessed.

In Tampa, Florida, Gerald Payne, a former construction contractor turned preacher who kept a loaded gun in his boot, used the name of God to steal $500 million from eighteen thousand believers. He built his Greater Ministries International specifically as a vehicle for fraud, setting his sights on fundamentalist Christians in rural Pennsylvania, Ohio, and Virginia. From one side of his mouth he quoted Luke 6:38: "Give, and it shall be given unto you." From the other he sold his flock herbal remedies to treat cancer and offered them investments — he called them "blessings" — that would double in just seventeen months. He also pledged them a future someday in an independent promised land, an ecclesiastical domain, where governments would have no jurisdiction.

In south Texas, two brothers, Bartholomew and Steven Stephens, set up the fraudulent website salvationarmyonline.org so they could steal money from people wishing to give to victims of Hurricane Katrina.

Unfortunately, they weren't the only ones hiding behind charity and human kindness. Within one week of the storm that devastated New Orleans and the surrounding region in 2005, the FBI reported more than four thousand websites had, all at once, gone live to help raise money for Katrina relief. Many were real. But most of them — the FBI says more than 60% — were bogus.

It was exactly the same after the January 2010 earthquake in Haiti. There were phishing scams, fraudulent sites set up to imitate genuine charities; virus scams, sites with Trojan horses and malware that, when downloaded, would wreak havoc with someone's computer or steal information from it; investment scams, emails touting stocks that would increase in value because the shares were tied to companies involved with goods or services that were somehow linked to the disaster; sales scams; emails flogging disaster-related products; and hate websites. The Internet was also flooded with millions of emails purporting to be from disaster relief officials looking for people to donate money, to earn money by processing insurance claims, to donate clothes, or otherwise aimed at stealing identities of victims. There were chain letters and pyramid schemes based on religion, benevolence, and disaster charities; emails offering to help relocate victims for a fee; repair scams, phony contractors looking for money or equipment to rebuild Haiti; auction scams that falsely promised you can help the less fortunate by bidding on this wonderful object; and emails that were designed to look as if they came from the Red Cross, asking for contributions of just $5. Mixed into all that are mass appeals by email, in blogs and in chat rooms for the London Bombings Victims Fund, Tsunami Disaster Appeal, UNICEF Relief, Feed the Hungry, Feed the Poor, the Homeless at Christmas; and a whole slew of good old-fashioned typical Nigerian scams, like the email from the widow of a

Hurricane Katrina victim hoping someone can help recoup her late husband's $35 million fortune that had suddenly been frozen in a nonexistent river delta bank.

How many television preachers have stolen fortunes from unselfish viewers by convincing them that "God wants you to send me your money"?

Altruism is an easy sell.

On street corners in New York, Chicago, Detroit, Los Angeles, Phoenix, Dallas, Miami, Atlanta, St. Louis, Kansas City, and thousands of other cities and towns across the country, well-dressed men and women carry buckets and hand out "I Gave" stickers with official-looking emblems — Victims of the Southern California Wildfires, Police Department, Fire Department, Support Our Overworked and Underpaid Troops, Association for Very Tall Disabled Veterans, School for Disabled Children, Hero Veterans of Iraq, Hero Veterans of Afghanistan, Unmarried Victims of 9/11, School for Blind Children, School for Deaf Children, Help for Seniors Relocating to Florida — all of them appealing to heartstrings, collecting money from generous citizens that they put straight into their own pockets because the charities don't really exist.

Payne was sentenced to twenty-seven

years. The Stephens brothers went to jail for nearly ten years each. But the folks on the street corners are still there. So are dozens of new Paynes and Stephens.

Your Best Defense

You need to know what you're giving to, and who. States and cities register charities, effectively licensing them, and require that they file annual reports to show you how your donation is used. Whether they're called the Charity Bureau, Registry of Charitable Organizations, the Office of Charities and Trusts, or the Division of Charitable Solicitations, they are the best source for information on the legitimacy of local and statewide charities.

In addition:

- The National Association of State Charity Officials publishes the directory of state charity offices online (www.nasconet.org/agencies).
- The Better Business Bureau is a good place to check on whether a charitable appeal is genuine (www.give.org).
- The American Institute of Philanthropy (www.charitywatch.org), the charity watchdog, is another good starting point.

- The IRS publishes lists of charities they have deemed worthy of tax-deductible donations under the heading "search for charities" (www.irs.gov/charities/article/0,,id=96136,00.html).
- The Federal Trade Commission (FTC) has detailed information on how to avoid charity fraud (www.ftc.gov/charityfraud).
- Charity Navigator, an independent evaluator, claims to be the nation's largest and most used assessor of charities (www.charitynavigator.org).

Because fraud based on benevolence is so ugly, and so deeply harmful by detouring money away from people and groups who truly need it, if you are willing to donate your money to a cause, you have the right to know that your money is going to good use. Accordingly:

- Beware of look-alikes. Con men often try to fool people with names and web addresses very similar to those of legitimate charities.
- Do not respond to unsolicited charitable appeals that arrive by email.
- Refuse to be pressured by aggressive cold callers. Telemarketing fraud, dis-

guised as a charity appeal, is more and more common. The best defense, if in doubt, is simply to hang up.

- Never follow a link from an email or website to another site. To ensure that contributions to nonprofit organizations are used for the intended purposes, go directly to the charity's website.
- Always verify the legitimacy of nonprofit organizations.
- Never open attachments in emails from unknown sources that claim to show pictures of a disaster area or victims. They may contain viruses.

Chapter Four:
Gullibility and Fear

Spot the difference:

After failing for ten years to take the city of Troy from the Trojans, the Greeks build a huge wooden horse, large enough for soldiers to hide inside, then place it outside the city's gates. Not knowing what to do with it, the Trojans wheel it inside the gates. The soldiers hidden in the wooden horse sneak out, open the city's gates, and the entire Greek army rushes in. The Trojans are decisively beaten.

The emperor loves clothes so much that he's willing to spend his fortune on the finest cloth. One day a merchant comes to him saying that the most expensive cloth in the world is invisible. Wanting nothing but the best, the emperor commands a suit be made for him with this invisible cloth, and proudly wears it at the next official parade. Because he says he can see his beautiful new suit, as he walks naked through the streets, all his subjects applaud, pretending that they can see it, too.

An email or official-looking letter arrives for you from U.S. Customs and Border Protection saying:

We hereby bring to your notice that a Diplomat with a consignment that was to be delivered to your residence has been stopped by us. This is as a result of the United States of America security measure to avert and combat any form of terrorism and money laundering through the sales of illegal drugs locally and internationally.

During our investigation, we found out that the consigment contained the sum of US$3.7 Million which upon further investigation revealed that the fund is your inheritance.

We have done our due diligence and have confirmed that you are legitimate beneficiary of the fund, and it is no threat to National Security. Consequently, your consignment will be delivered at your residence by the diplomat without delay after all protocols have been duly observed.

During our interrogation on why this fund was not transferred to your bank account, the diplomat revealed that some people

75

want to divert your inheritance fund, so he decided to act fast by moving the fund through this means. We hereby advise you to discontinue any further dealings with any other person.

However, before the delivery is made we need you to reconfirm the following information, so that the delivery will be made accurately.

Full Name:
Residential Address:
Date of Birth:
Occupation:
Telephone/Mobile Numbers:

We await your response. Regards, Thomas S. Winkowski, Assistant Commissioner, Office of Field Operations, U.S. Customs and Border Protection

Spot the difference yet?
If you have, you're working too hard.
There is no difference.

GULLIBILITY

Reread the letter that's supposed to be from U.S. Customs and Border Protection. If it doesn't sound quite right that's because it isn't quite right. It certainly doesn't sound official. And anyway, Americans don't talk like that.

Now think about this — if someone were stopped at the border with all that cash, wouldn't the government take the time to send a couple of agents to your house to ask what's going on? Since when does law enforcement accept at face value something as overtly suspicious as a suitcase stuffed with hundred-dollar bills? Furthermore, U.S. law states that anyone entering the country with more than $10,000 in cash or financial instruments must declare it at the port of entry. Having heard every excuse under the sun for every infraction possible, border patrol officers don't accept half-baked stories even when it's only $10,001. Do you really think they're going to say, welcome, step right in, everything's dandy for $3.7 million?

Scams like that — sometimes put under the general heading of windfall or inheritance fraud — all rely on basic gullibility.

- The heir to a huge fortune chooses you, out of the blue, to help him clear up some legal difficulties surrounding his inheritance. In return, he will happily share his inheritance with you.
- Someone has luckily stumbled across

a fortune secretly salted away by
_____ (fill in the blank with Josef
Stalin, Charles Darwin, Sir Francis
Drake, former Indonesian president
Suharto, former Philippine president
Ferdinand Marcos, Babe Ruth, Elvis,
Michael Jackson, whoever) and needs
help recouping it before the rightful
heirs find out. Shh, don't tell anyone.
If you want half, you have to help cover
the expenses.

- My great aunt died intestate and her
lawyer says that if I, her only living
relative, am going to get the $7 million
she's left behind, he needs to put
someone's name in her will as sole
benefactor. If you're willing to do this,
my lawyer's willing to send you the
money. But first, because I'm being so
generous as to cut you in, I'm afraid
you'll have to pay his expenses.

Pull these scams apart, dissect them —
the way you should any offer that seems too
good to be true — and they unravel all too
easily. They just don't make sense. In fact,
when you scrutinize these claims closely,
they might even be laughable. But the con
man is counting on you reading it only
once, on gullibility taking hold quickly, and

78

the careless excitement that inevitably follows leading you into doing something foolish.

THE FEAR FACTOR

Every successful fraudster knows what buttons to push because that's how he earns his living. Now add to greed, benevolence, and gullibility the button labeled "fear."

Fear of failure can prod many students to cram for finals, fear of fines can keep some drivers within the speed limit, and fear of potential tragedy definitely drives the sale of home smoke detectors.

But fear not only motivates action, it can also create inaction. Fear can generate a panic that freezes us in our own footsteps and overrides clear thinking. That's why con men push that button. Wrapping fear with confusion and a sense of urgency — this must happen right now, or else! — heightens anxiety to produce a deer-caught-in-the-headlights result. And that can give a fraudster just enough time to take control of the situation. He incites panic and then, without allowing his victim time to think about the illogic of his plight, offers a fast, almost logical solution.

Fear Meets a Windfall Inheritance

In one of the more popular inheritance frauds, you're sternly warned that not answering questions is actually against the law:

- To collect this windfall, the law requires you to fill out an Origin of Funds Certificate (OFC), proving that the funds have no links with any form of illegality.

- Failure to pay the required fees is confirmation that you intended to violate the Patriot Act and a federal offense.

- Any breach of secrecy is a breach of the Last Will and Testament Act, as defined by state law, and immediately invalidates any claim to the money.

- In accordance with U.S. codes governing international transfers of inherited assets, you will be required to purchase and pay for, in advance, an International Inherited Assets importation fee of $250, the sum of which must be wired within five days to the referral officer in charge, name as noted, of the European Union (EEC) International Inherited Assets Importation Office, in care of the Western Union office, address as noted, in Brussels, Belgium.

Fear and Your Civic Duty

In jury duty fraud, the fear factor is used to panic citizens who have never broken a law in their life.

An official-looking letter or email arrives with your name and address clearly spelled out. It claims to come from some official-sounding body — Bailiff of the State Court, Jury Summons Office, Jury Administrative Office, Clerk of the Court, Judicial District Jury Office, Office of Jury Commissioner, whatever. Next to your name and address there is a case number, and near that a return address, which is often a post office box. There is also a phone number, which, when you call it, turns out to be an answering machine.

The message explains how sometime ago — usually 90 to 120 days — a notice was sent to you requiring your presence on a jury. In every state of the Union, when you're notified to serve on a jury, you are legally obliged to respond. This notice says that when you failed to respond, a second notice was issued. When you failed to respond to that, a third notice was sent, allowing you a fixed amount of time — say

14 days — to explain to the court why you disregarded those previous notices. Furthermore, the third notice clearly spelled out that should you fail to respond this time, an arrest warrant would be issued.

Now, the message says that having failed to provide a suitable explanation for your absence, a warrant has indeed been issued for your arrest. The charge is noted as either contempt of court or failure to appear. In either case, you are informed, you are subject to immediate arrest, and a guilty verdict at trial can carry with it jail time.

You cry, "But I'm innocent!"

Which is precisely what the fraudster is counting on.

Faced with something as sudden and dramatic as the possibility of going to jail, very few people have the presence of mind to think this through: I was not previously summoned for jury duty, because if I had been, I would have received the official notice by mail. After all, they knew how to reach me with this. How come they didn't find me with the previous three notices? And, do the courts really operate this way?

Instead, all you can think of is, I'm a fugitive.

Given this predictable result, the fraudster has provided you with a convenient solution. The notice says, if the warrant has been issued in error — you think, *Damn right it has* — you should go to our website, or phone our special jury hotline number, and provide sufficient proof of your innocence.

So you make a beeline for the escape hatch. To prove that you're you and not the person named on the arrest warrant, the website or the hotline requires personal information: name, address, phone, birth date, mother's maiden name, Social Security number, banking and credit card details, and so on. And in your panic, you hand the con man exactly what he needs.

While letters and email are what's commonly used in this scam, some fraudsters have taken to the phone to inform potential victims of the arrest warrant. They identify themselves as officers of the court, sometimes even using the real name of a person working in a real court office. They admonish you for missing jury duty — or, in one variation, they announce that they are giving you yet another chance, but need to pre-screen prospective jurors — and go through the same scenario as the website and hotline, demanding personal information. Should you balk at giving them that information, they threaten not just arrest but also the possibility of steep fines.

In one simple variation, you can be excused from having missed jury duty and the arrest warrant will be dropped, if you agree to pay a fine using your credit card. But it has to be right now. Any delay will put you in further jeopardy.

Of course, if you take the time to look closely, you should see through this. Names and addresses of prospective jurors usually come from voter registration lists, so jury offices already have your name and address. And that's all they need. Contact between the courts and prospective jurors comes through the mail. No one is summoned for jury duty by email. Nor do court officials phone people who have missed jury duty. Only con men do that.

There is nothing about jury duty that requires you to divulge your mother's maiden name, your bank account number, or your credit card information. Nothing whatsoever! And in some rare instance when phone contact with a genuine court official is necessary, you will never be asked for personal or sensitive information.

But fear is extremely effective. It's a rare person who, when faced with this, is cool and collected enough to do the easiest, simplest, and most obvious thing: Go to a phone book or ask information for the

number of the real clerk of the real court —
never call a phone number provided in an
unsolicited email, letter, or phone call —
and ask him, what's this all about?

Fear is the motivation behind such frauds
as:

- Text messages from your bank announcing that your account has been
closed due to suspicious activities. You
are instructed to dial an 800 number,
after which you're asked to verify your
account number and password, obviously so that the scammers can clean
it out.
- Email from a company that intends to
foreclose on your home and then demands a fee to stop it.
- Someone pretending to be your credit
card company saying there's been a
serious breach and you will need to
reactivate your card by telling them
your card number and new password.
- Someone pretending to be a police
officer investigating a crime who needs
you to identify yourself to his satisfaction, which includes your Social Security number, mother's maiden name,
and bank account information.

For the Sake of a Quarter in the Meter

Fear is also the driving factor behind the quirky, sometimes very dangerous, phony parking ticket scam.

In various cities around California, sham tickets have shown up on windshields of high-end cars. Fines range from $100 to $500. A note explains how to pay online using a credit card or via PayPal. Obviously, people who can't be bothered to argue about fines have been paying them.

In other places around the country, including Washington, DC, phony tickets offer a 50% discount for prompt payment, encouraging people to pay online and get it over with, rather than fight it and — at least they believe — risk a higher fine.

In Boulder, Colorado, a few years ago, tickets appeared on cars with instructions to pay the fine by check directly to the Boulder Police Department. But anyone who took the time to verify the address would see that the one listed on the ticket was not the police department's.

In Madison, Wisconsin, a local university student named Anthony Gallagher printed tickets with the logo "Capitol and Isthmus District Parking Enforcement" — a phony name, which should have been a giveaway — and handed them out, demanding $40 per violation. He used a post office box to collect payments and opened a special bank account to deposit the money. He worked his scam for six weeks and reportedly collected several hundred dollars before the local cops shut him down.

While these examples represent elementary theft, in Grand Forks, North Dakota, the fraud-by-fear phony parking ticket scam took on a much more sinister guise. There, tickets were placed on cars legally parked at malls, hospitals, and supermarkets, with the notice, "This vehicle is in violation of standard parking regulations." Farther down the very official-looking ticket, there was a website address where the supposed violators could view pictures that proved the infraction.

Incensed that they'd been ticketed when there was no obvious violation, many of the people who received these tickets went quickly to the website. Once there, they were instructed that, in order to see the photos of their poorly parked car, they had to download a small program called PictureSearchToolbar.

And there-in lay the real scam. Instead of a toolbar, victims unknowingly downloaded a Trojan horse which installed some malware — malicious software — that reported a security flaw in the owner's computer. To get rid of it, victims were instructed to buy a certain antivirus software program for $50, which also turned out to be phony.

At the same time, the malware is said to have had the capability of capturing user keystrokes which could reveal online passwords and account numbers. It also, apparently, installed a "bot" — a web robot — that could provide remote access to the victim's computer.

Your Best Defense

When gullibility and fear are the cards the fraudster is playing, your best defense is time. Con men will do everything they can to rush you, because that's in their interest. You need time — and must take the time — to calm down, collect your thoughts, and react in a sensible manner.

To determine if a threat to you is legitimate or simply aimed at provoking fear:

- Never answer any questions right away. Tell the person who has contacted you that you will get back in touch as soon as possible — be prepared for him to resist that — then use the phone book or the Internet to find a genuine number for the office where this person

88

supposedly works. Call there and request to speak, by name, with that person.

- If the letter, email, or phone call appears to be legitimate, consider the fact that:
  - The person on the other end will have a legitimate office address and a legitimate phone number. Do not respond to a P.O. Box or assume that an 800 number is legitimate.
  - The person on the other end will have a legitimate email or web address. Government and police addresses typically end in dot-gov. They do not use dot-com. What's more, officials and employees — whether you're talking about a court clerk, an investigator, or someone who works in a bank — will not be using an AOL, Gmail, Yahoo! or Hotmail address.
- If the person on the other end is legitimate, he or she already knows who you are and doesn't need to ask you for that information again. Therefore, when someone in authority insists he needs to verify your personal data,

turn the situation around. Have him read back to you the data he already has on file so that you can verify that.

CHAPTER FIVE:
IDENTITY THEFT

Sometimes referred to as the fastest-growing felony in the world, identity theft is also certainly one of the most insidious. Crimes are committed in your name — more often than not, you are also one of the victims — and, at the same time, you're left to clean up the mess.

While the Internet has vastly increased the spread of the crime and been the singular most important reason why identity thieves often go unpunished — anonymity is synonymous with the Internet — it is hardly anything new.

Long before the World Wide Web and email, criminals realized that the easiest way to commit a crime against you was by obtaining enough information about you to become you. They could also commit crimes against other people while disguised as you. It began with finding out who you were, and the most efficient way to do that was the old-fashioned way — by stealing your wallet, your mail, or your garbage.

Your wallet has your credit cards, the mail brings checkbooks, bank statements, and applications for preapproved credit cards, and, as for your garbage, you are what you throw away.

In the days before you could buy a use-at-home, confetti-cut shredder for less than $50, you threw away bank statements, credit card statements, utility bills, used checks, personal stationery, old bills, and old prescriptions. You tossed out old paperwork with your signature, Social Security number, insurance number, birth date, names of your family members with their birth dates and their Social Security numbers, and all sorts of business-related paperwork. Okay, you crumpled it up or ripped everything in half, or maybe you did both, but that never stopped anybody. It was dead easy to put enough of your identity back together to apply for new credit cards in your name, to run up bills in stores in your name, and to inform your bank that you are changing your address so that your checks and bank statements would be diverted and someone could go to town on your money, leaving you to clean up the mess.

Life for the crooks changed to a large

extent with the advent of shredders and the Internet. They stopped hanging around your neighborhood to rummage through your garbage and, instead, hung out wherever they wanted to, rummaging through the information that you are invariably leaving all over the digital world. And if you aren't willingly leaving enough, they've come up with ways to trick you into leaving more.

The Federal Trade Commission (FTC) estimates that nine million Americans will have their identities stolen this year. Fraudsters will try to rob your credit card numbers when you use your card. They will pretend to be your bank and get you to leave your account number and password on a phony website. They will call you and ask for the information, or write you and ask for the information. They will then misuse your credit card, write checks on your bank account, sell copies of your driver's license, use your Social Security number to open more accounts that they can misuse, obtain your birth certificate which they can easily sell into the huge illegal aliens market, get a job with your Social Security number, take out a mortgage or rent a property with your identity, obtain all sorts of services including medical and dental, use your name and ID when they get into trouble with the police, and even file for a tax refund as you.

Chances are you won't realize that any of this is happening until after it happens and, then, sometimes until it's much too late to save yourself.

TEN ESSENTIAL THINGS TO DO IMMEDIATELY IF YOUR IDENTITY IS STOLEN

If you fall victim to identity theft, time is against you. Fraudsters who perpetuate these crimes are counting on you being disbelieving ("This can't be happening to me"), upset, disorganized, and unable to act promptly. They know that the more time you give them, the more they can steal.

The first thing you need to do is limit the damage. That means getting your good name back as soon as possible. The longer you wait, the greater the damage.

Fraudsters are betting you won't go through all ten of these steps. If you don't, you're just making their job easier.

Follow the checklist in this order:

1. **Notify all the financial institutions you do business with.** Tell your banks, your mortgage lender, plus all the various issuers of credit cards, debit cards, store cards that

you hold — even ones you don't normally use — that you've had your identity stolen. Insist that they immediately cancel all of your accounts and issue you with new ones. Write down the name of the person you're speaking with, plus the date and time of the call. Then insist that they send you written confirmation of your call, noting that your account has been closed as of the time and date of your call. If you don't receive confirmation in a few days, phone back and harass them until they send it. (*Note:* If you haven't fallen victim to identity theft and you don't yet have a complete list of your personal banking and credit card information — including account numbers and phone numbers to call in just such an emergency — make one now. Be sure to hide it in a safe place.)

2. **Notify all other creditors in the same way.** This includes utility companies, telephone companies, Internet providers, your cell phone provider, cable TV and Wi-Fi provider, schools, stores, anyone and everyone who sends you regular

bills. Again, you should already have a list prepared, just in case.

3. **Contact the various credit reporting agencies and ask them to issue a fraud alert.** Credit reporting agencies should send you a form to fill out so that you can explain what's happened, which they will then add to your credit history. At the same time, you need to tell them that you're opting out of any preapproved credit card and insurance offers in order to stop someone else from opening new credit card/debit card accounts in your name. Again, write down the name of the person you're speaking with, plus the time and date of the call. And demand written confirmation. Then, insist that the reporting agency send you a revised credit report, which must include the fact that you duly alerted them to the fraud so that you can see if any creditors have had unauthorized requests. You will find contact information for the credit reporting agencies in "Resources" at the back of the book.

4. **If the revised credit report**

shows that there have been un-authorized requests for new accounts in your name, get straight back to those creditors. Notify the creditors in writing that accounts have been tampered with or opened without your knowledge. Ask the agency to provide you with copies of any documents showing fraudulent transactions. If they refuse to provide them to you, get a name, address, and phone number of a responsible person at the agency who can then be contacted by the police. Keep copies of all correspondence and make sure you get a written response to everything you send them.

5. **Notify the police.** File a fraud complaint. The reason that notifying the police is not the first step is because you need to give them more than just a story. The officer dealing with your case is looking for documentation. Without it, there is nothing much he can do. He needs copies of all the correspondence and reports you've already made, plus any information you've gleaned back from financial institutions and

credit reporting agencies. The more you can give the officer — especially names and numbers of people to contact — the easier his job will be and the more likely he is to pursue it. Be sure to take the name and phone number of the officer investigating your case. Ask him or her for a copy of the report you've filed, keep a copy for your own files, and send each — along with the officer's name and contact details — to all the financial institutions you do business with, plus all the credit reporting agencies.

6. **Notify everyone else who holds personal records on you.** This includes the DMV, the passport office, local and state government offices, the voter registration office, your insurance company, the IRS, Medicare, the City Hall Registrar's Office which issues birth certificates, your doctor, your HMO, schools, and libraries. Also, notify every company you've authorized for automatic payments from your bank account or regular charges to a credit card, such as Internet service providers, cable television, and

phone company. Send them each a letter explaining that you are a victim of identity theft, mention the police report number and the name and location of the investigating officer, and ask that all of your accounts — your driver's license, passport, anything and everything that connects your name to your address be shut and that new accounts be opened. Furthermore, remind them that any requests for information — such as a request for a copy of your birth certificate — should trigger an alarm bell and the police should be notified. It's a major pain in the neck to reconstitute your life, but you need to do it before the fraudster does.

7. **Go to your local post office with a letter addressed to the postal inspectors, explaining the situation and saying that your mail is not to be redirected.** One of the things that fraudsters find they can do, easily, is use your ID to redirect your mail. That allows them to identify your debtors and creditors, and tap into them. Explain in your letter to the postal inspectors that

you have been a victim of identity theft and that should any request for a change of address come in, the police should be notified immediately. Insist on written confirmation that your letter has been received. If you go a day or two without mail, call the post office and find out why.

8. **Radically change your Internet life.** Change every account name, user name, password, and PIN wherever you've got them. This means not just online banking sites, but also sites where you check your billing — such as phone companies and utilities — plus online auctions, online payment systems, online shopping sites. Wherever you need to log on, change it. And this time, stay away from the obvious. Do not use numbered equivalents of your name, your mother's maiden name, your phone number, or anything that so blatantly points to you or your family. Varied and random is harder to remember, but also harder to crack.

9. **Clean out all of your computers.** There are several very reputable antivirus, anti-spyware, anti-hacker

programs on the market. Norton and McAfee are probably the most popular, but they're not the only ones. AdAware and Spybot Search & Destroy are both free, download-able, and effective. Use as much as you can of the highly reputable programs to clean your computer of all the dangers that may be lurking in your RAM or on your hard drive. Once your computer is clean, keep it clean. Set up firewalls. Regularly use antivirus programs. Regularly clean out cache files. If you use Windows, regularly clean out your "prefetch" file. And change your email address so that anything the identity thief now throws at you never comes through.

10. **Stay in touch.** It's not over until the fat lady sings. And if she's the one who's stolen your identity, don't count on an aria very soon. Just because you've taken steps one through nine, that's not the end of the problem. You need to stay in touch with all of the financial institutions and reporting agencies you've already notified. Identity thieves are persistent. If they can't

get into one of your accounts the first time, they will try a second and a third and a fourth time. What's more, if they have already gotten inside an account, you can count on the fact that they will be back for seconds.

It is important to know that the only time the law requires you to divulge your Social Security number is when a company needs it for tax matters, Social Security, Medicare, and other government purposes. You are not obliged to hand it out to anyone who insists on having it, nor should you let them have it. If you feel that someone has misused or is misusing your Social Security number fraudulently, notify the Social Security Administration immediately. (See "Resources" for contact information.)

It's a little-known fact that you can ask the Social Security Administration to change your SSN. They won't let you do it just to escape a bad credit rating. But they will do it if you fit their fraud victim criteria.

CHAPTER SIX:
SMALLER THAN A 2¢ PHONE CALL
CYBERFRAUD

The world became a radically different place the day a computer first hooked up to a modem, shrinking the planet to smaller than a 2¢ phone call. Suddenly you could talk to, and send files to, and buy from, and sell to, and get in touch with anyone in the wired universe. Thanks to the anonymity of the web, fraudsters could hide somewhere in the Third World and defraud folks in the First.

The planet got even smaller as broadband, Wi-Fi, laptops, BlackBerrys, and iPhones put real-time communications — email, news, weather, sports, and porn — into our pockets and briefcases. Now fraudsters could hide in plain sight and became, virtually, invisible.

Where once there was no such thing as a perfect crime, suddenly the planet is overflowing with perfect crimes. If you are so inclined, you can sip mint juleps on your

balcony overlooking the French Riviera —
or in the bustle of downtown Bangkok, or
in the heat of Lagos Nigeria, or in the ruins
of the Soviet Empire somewhere in Kazakh-
stan — and tap into other people's computers to empty their bank accounts, buy from
them and never pay, sell to them and never
deliver, or just become someone else and
run amok with other people's money.

Some of the information crooks need to
steal your identity is easy enough for anyone
to find. Google yourself and you may be
very surprised to see what's openly available. Once, while looking for an old friend
from years ago, a basic Google search
turned up his daughter's husband's golf
scores and, not far from that, their unlisted
home phone number. It doesn't take a
genius to find things most of us thought
were unfindable.

But much of what anyone can find out
about you is information that you wind up
giving them. It's the two-way street crime
syndrome.

In this case it's called phishing and pharming, and both can be disastrous.

PHISHING
Phishing is the act of luring you onto a website that you believe is the right one but is,

104

in fact, a fake.

It begins with an email that you think is from your bank. It looks exactly like the real thing and announces that there is some sort of problem with your account. For instance, it says that the bank has received a written request to issue a check for a substantial sum to someone you never heard of. The email explains that the request seemed odd to the managers who suspect that something is wrong, and so before they do anything they want to make sure this is an authorized transaction. Accordingly, they ask you to log on to the bank's website and verify your account. And to make it easy, they've provided a link to the site.

Except the link goes to a dummy site that belongs to the fraudsters but looks exactly like the real thing. There, you log in with your account name, account number, and password and, as soon as you do, you've handed the fraudsters access to your account.

It took the bad guys a while to figure this out, because they had to learn how to replicate a genuine website. Throughout the late 1990s, they made obvious mistakes, like spelling and grammar. But just into the new century, they got it right and perpetrated one of the most famous phishing scams of all time.

PLEASE VERIFY YOUR INFORMATION

Dear PayPal Member,
Your account has been randomly flagged in our system as part of our routine security measures. This is a must to ensure that only you have access and use of your PayPal account and to ensure a safe PayPal experience.

We require all flagged accounts to verify their information on file with us. To verify your information <u>click here</u> and enter the details requested.

After you verify your information, your account shall be returned to good standing and you will continue to have full use of your account. Thank you for using PayPal.

Most people had never seen anything like this. It came from a legitimate PayPal address — although at the bottom of the email it said do not respond to this address — and because so many people believed it, they hit the "click here" link, which took them to a page that looked exactly like the genuine PayPal log-in screen.

The success of that scam pretty much set the standard for all the phishing crimes that have followed. And these days, the bad guys really know what they're doing. These days it's very difficult to spot the fraudulent site. *Consumer Reports* claims that more than seven million end users — one home in thirteen — divulged sensitive details to phishers during 2007–2008. The URL cgi-paypal.us is not PayPal, the URL chase .onlinecustomer.info is not Chase, and the return address onlinebanking@alert.bankof america.com has nothing to do with the Bank of America. Once upon a time you could check the status bar at the bottom of your screen and see the little lock that indicates the website is secure. But they've learned how to fake those, too.

A phishing email from AOL says your bill needs to be adjusted and sends you to bill .aol.com, which is not an AOL site. An email from Citibank to say your account has been suspended uses a link to business access.citibank.citigroup.com, which is not a Citibank site.

While barclays.validation.co.uk has nothing to do with Barclays Bank — that's the link the fraudsters use in one of their phishing emails — every now and then the fraudsters figure the average person wouldn't know how to spot a fake anyway. So a message from SunTrust Bank in Florida to say that they've just completed a scheduled maintenance of their servers that requires you to reconfirm your password directs you to a URL ending with .ru, which is Russia.

Another difference between then and now is, in the beginning, the con men were greedy enough to empty your account right away. Today they're smart enough to leave it alone. They email back that the problem is resolved, reassuring you that it was a bank error that caused their concerns and that everything is now okay. But over the course of the following weeks, they begin to use whatever additional information they've been able to glean by watching your account, to order credit cards in your name, open other accounts in your name, perhaps even take out a mortgage in your name. The amount of money they're able to steal that way far outweighs the money you may have in your account at any given time.

PHARMING

Phishing's nasty little cousin pharming happens when a malicious code is installed on your personal computer — usually through an email or an attachment that you've downloaded — which misdirects you to fraudulent websites without your knowledge. Once it's in place, every time you try to go to the genuine site of, say, American Express, you'll be redirected to the scammer's fraudulent American Express site. Or, if the fraudsters are really clever, you will be allowed to go to the genuine site, but then a pop-up screen — triggered by the malware — will ask for your personal information.

YOUR BEST DEFENSE

Whenever fraud is concerned, your best and first line of defense should be common sense. Always ask yourself, why does this person need this information? And, do I know for sure that this person is who he says he is?

Protecting yourself from phishing and pharming attacks means properly arming your computer. You should have software installed that blocks pop-ups, spam filters for your email, a firewall, plus antivirus and anti-spyware software. And you need to keep them up-to-date. There is no guarantee that you will then be safe, but you will certainly be safer with all of that than without it.

The scammers understand this, and are now fighting fire with fire. Because people are more and more aware of the necessity to protect themselves with software, the bad guys have a second act — fake security and maintenance software upgrades.

An email that looks like it's from one of the big anti-spam, antivirus, anti-spyware companies — and even Microsoft — announces that an antispam, antivirus, anti-spyware upgrade is available. You're given a link for the download and when you click on it, the upgrade turns out to be malware that starts the whole pharming process over again.

To counter the dangers posed by both phishing and pharming attacks, read emails from companies carefully. If it talks about your account, and you don't have an account with that company, then you know to throw it away. If it is from someone at a company with whom you do business, but doesn't contain your name and some hint of your account number, then this one is also fake. If you have a relationship with a company, and they need to send you an email, they will address you by name. If PayPal sends you an email addressed "Dear PayPal User," it's phony. Same goes for all the hundreds of banks that are used by scammers to lure you into a trap. Receiving an email from Bank of America or Citibank addressed to anything but your name should be binned. So, too, the airlines and their frequent flyer clubs. They know your name and account number, and that's how they address their emails. A note addressed to "Dear Valued Frequent Flyer" definitely is not from the airline.

Your scam radar should be on full alert:

- If the email asks you to click on a link to verify your account information, it's fake. Legitimate companies never do that.
- If you are asked to disclose your password or any financial information by email, because no legitimate company would request you to.

Also:

- Look at email addresses and URLs carefully. If you're suspicious, Google the address or URL inside quotation marks and see what happens. Many fraudulent addresses and URLs will show up on anti-scam websites.
- Beware of pop-up screens. Some legitimate sites may use them, but they never use them to obtain personal information.

- Be extremely suspicious of attachments. If you receive an email with an attachment that you're not expecting, or an attachment from someone you don't know, never open it. Even if it does come from someone you know, it can still be hiding malware. Also, banks and financial institutions never send emails with attachments to update software. Anything even remotely like that is a scam.
- Keep your email address off scammers lists in two very simple ways. First, never post your address in a public forum. Con men use software to hunt down anything with an @ symbol. If you have to list your address, write it out as "at." Second, never opt out of an unsolicited email. They almost always have links saying that if you don't want to hear from them again, just click here. But in the case of scammers, that merely tells them that your address is live.

Phishing attacks can come through the phone, too. If it's your bank or credit card company legitimately contacting you about a transaction, they will only ask about that transaction. They won't ask for your account number and password. If it's a con man, he'll ask for everything.

HOW TO SPOT A SCAM EMAIL

Spotting the difference between the real thing and a phony is easy when you know what to look for. If you answer yes to even one of the following twelve questions, the email is a con. Do not respond. Delete it.

1. Has the email been addressed to "undisclosed recipients"?

2. Is it from a high official in a foreign government, agency, or business, when you don't happen to know any high officials in foreign governments, agencies, or businesses?

3. Does the salutation read something like Dear Beloved, Dear Valued Friend, Valued Customer, or anything even remotely like it?

4. Is it from a company you have never done business with, such as a bank where you don't have an account?

5. Is it from a company you have done business with, such as a bank, but is asking you to verify your account or provide personal information?

6. Are there spelling and grammar mistakes?

Is the message sometimes difficult to grasp? Is it supposed to be official and yet doesn't sound official?

7. Is this about a business deal where the sender is looking for a partner or someone to help him in a highly lucrative venture? Are there assurances that it is risk free and absolutely on the level? Are the sums involved so much that you think this can't be true?

8. Does he promise to give you all the details later but refuses to go into any details until you respond with personal details?

9. Is there any mention of Nigeria or another country in West Africa?

10. Does the sender refer to where you live as "your country"?

11. Does the tale he's spinning seem odd and convoluted?

12. Is anyone asking you to send money on the promise that if you do, you will receive back a much larger sum?

BUY, SELL, CHEAT, LIE, STEAL

According to the Internet Crime Complaint Center (www.ic3.gov) — a joint venture of the FBI, the National White Collar Crime Center (www.nw3c.org), and the Bureau of Justice Assistance (www.ojp.usdoj.gov/bja) — cybercrime has been increasing at the astonishing rate of nearly 50% a year for the past several years. It gives truth to the maxim that when the economy goes down, crime goes up.

For several years, the number one crime in cyberspace has been online auction fraud. But the center recently revised the list, and these days it's transaction fraud, in which people don't deliver merchandise or payment. Both crimes are excellent examples of how the Internet is the ideal first choice for fraudsters. But both crimes also show how specific cybercrimes still work in the real world.

First, the online version.

You win something on eBay, pay for it, but the seller never ships it. That's fraud. You sell something on eBay, collect the money, and don't bother sending it. That's fraud. Some sellers list counterfeit items, with sports memorabilia autographs being high on that list. Same goes for counterfeit art, stamps, antiques, and other collectibles. Or someone buys something, claims it was never received, and tries to get his money back. That's also fraud.

Some sellers are interested in using an online auction only to get into your credit card or PayPal account. Some buyers deliberately overpay, using the purchase to steal what you've just sold them and, at the same time, to run an overpayment check fraud scam on the back of the sale.

A phishing email purports to come from an eBay seller, saying "I tried to contact you but no answer. You are the winning bidder of my auction. Respond to me or else I will contact eBay and give you negative feedback."

You check the attached item number and see a computer, a DVD recorder, or a part for a car you don't own. But none of that matters because you know you didn't bid on it. However, there is a link to click on which will, supposedly, take you to another eBay location where you can explain to the company that you didn't bid on this. Of course, the link is not eBay's. And there, thinking you're canceling the purchase, the fraudster gets you to give up your personal account information.

Another eBay scam works off the "second chance" system for items you bid on but didn't win.

The seller has used a "shill account" — one that he controls but with a different name, address, and credit card attached — to bid up his item. If someone buys it at the inflated price, that's fine with him. But if it doesn't sell, he turns to the second chance system that eBay has put in place to increase sales. He explains to the underbidder that the winner backed out of the sale so he can now offer it at the shill inflated price. If the underbidder takes the deal, that's what the seller wanted all along. If he doesn't, the seller can always negotiate down to the underbidder's last bid.

Underbidders should suspect that something is wrong if the seller offers you the item right away. Apparently most second chance offers take place at least a week after the auction ends.

Other commonly used online auction frauds include

- **Misrepresentation.** The item described isn't the item on sale. Con men lie about values, size, origin, authentication, and condition. Add into this piracy, counterfeiting, and forgeries.
- **Fencing.** Online auctions are the perfect place to sell stolen goods. The honest buyer's problem is that the purchase of stolen goods is just as illegal as the sale of stolen goods, and even if the purchase is honest — the buyer did not know the item was stolen — he still risks losing it and also losing whatever he paid for it.
- **Switch Fraud.** You sell something on-

line, the buyer pays for it, and you ship it. But the buyer returns the item claiming it's damaged or not as described. He demands a refund. It's only when you look closely at the returned item that you see it's not the same as the one you sent him. It is damaged or it's simply a fake. It becomes a dispute between you, the buyer, and the online auction house, and, in most cases, you lose. The buyer keeps the good item and gets his money back.

- **Triangle Fraud.** You purchase an item on approval. The con man seller pays for shipping it to you with a stolen credit card. You are then required to pay for the item with a money transfer. When the police eventually get involved, the money trail from the stolen credit card leads to you, not the con man.

The offline version works pretty much the same way.

You've listed your old wide-screen television for sale on Craigslist, and a message comes back from a potential buyer. He says he wants the set, and to convince you that he's a serious buyer, he is even willing to pay you an extra $100 if you take the listing down so that he can be certain you won't sell it out from under him to someone else at a higher price.

He says that he will take care of the shipping but needs your name, address, and phone number so that he can get a bank check to you overnight. You supply it, and he says the check is on the way. Then comes a call or email explaining a slight error. The buyer says his secretary made a mistake, and instead of sending the bank check for $650, she made it out for $950.

It's the standard overpayment scam.

Either he asks you to wire the difference to a phony address, supposedly to cover the shipping, or simply to wire the difference back to him. When your bank notifies you that the check is counterfeit, you're out the item plus the money you wired back.

The way to avoid it, of course, is not to reimburse overpayments until the check actually clears, and then never to ship goods until they've been properly paid for.

Whenever you're buying or selling, online or through a free paper like Craigslist:

- Do not wire payments or, especially, overpayments with Western Union, MoneyGram, or any other service. If at all possible, use a credit card because that offers you some insurance against theft.

- If you possibly can, always deal locally. Being able to meet the buyer or seller will help you avoid most of these scams.
- Do not believe any claim that the on-line auction house or a free paper, like Craigslist, will guarantee a transaction. They are middlemen. They do not handle payments, certify buyers or sellers, provide escrow services, or offer any buyer or seller protection. Emails from eBay or Craigslist or any middleman offering a guarantee are fakes.

Along these same lines, a recent scam going through the free papers is the apartment rental hustle and is based on the experience con men have gained working online auction fraud. You advertise an apartment for rent, and an email comes in from someone in another country to accept the offer, sight unseen. You're delighted the apartment moved so fast and happy to do your new tenant a little favor. He says that he will send you the security deposit and the first month's rent, but needs to get his furniture and personal property delivered and asks if he can include the money he has to pay for that. Just cash the check and wire the difference to the shipping company.

Again, the overpayment scam.

There being nothing new under the sun, the seller's version is the out-of-town key scam.

You've found an apartment you want, either in an ad or at an online bulletin board, but the landlord claims that he lives out of town. However, he's happy to let you see the place. Except that the keys are out of town, too. So, he says, if you put down a security deposit, he'll mail you the keys. If you take the apartment, keep the keys and he'll credit your security deposit against whatever payments are due. If you don't want the place, you return the keys and he'll return your money.

Don't hold your breath. The Better Business Bureau (BBB) has been reporting that some scammers who advertise in free papers claim they are businesses accredited by the BBB, or that the listing is covered by the BBB's buyer participation plan.

You can get the same guarantees from online auction escrow sites run by scammers.

Understand that the BBB does not have any buyer protection plans, that anyone claiming the BBB will guarantee a purchase is a crook, and that online auction escrow sites need to be checked out very carefully. The same goes for anyone who insists that victims of Internet fraud can file for a reimbursement from the Internet Crime Complaint Center. It's not true.

In the end, the key to protecting yourself when doing any business online is always to assume the worst:

- Check sellers before you buy.
- Check buyers before you sell.
- Understand that the farther away the buyer or seller is, the more difficult it will be to collect if something goes wrong.
- If you are going to use an escrow service, check it out thoroughly.
- Insure deliveries for everything, including damage.
- If there is a problem on eBay, inform them and then try to settle your differences with their mediation service.
- And never take someone else's word for his own honesty.

CHAPTER SEVEN:
GENIES IN BOTTLES
KNOWING WHO TO TRUST

At some point, just about everybody has been asked this question: What would you wish for?

You know the story — you're walking along a deserted beach, find a bottle, open it, and out pops a genie who says, "I have been trapped inside that bottle for a thousand years, and because you saved me, I shall grant you three wishes."

So, what would you wish for?

Many people go straight for the money. I want ten million bucks. I want a hundred million. Second and third wishes typically have to do with fame, great sex, big cars, big houses, big boats, big diamonds, big achievements. I want to be a movie star. I want to sleep with a movie star. I want a Rolls-Royce. I want to win the Super Bowl and be MVP.

Occasionally, some smart aleck comes up with, "And my third wish is . . . ten more wishes."

But no one ever seems to say, "What are you talking about? Genies in bottles don't exist."

That's because most of us like to believe in genies.

The fat man certainly didn't look like a genie. And the fact that he weighed 450 pounds meant it would have been one helluva bottle. But Alec (aka Alex) William Herbage had all the trappings of a genie who'd granted himself a lot of wishes.

He had a castle in Scotland, and the sixty-acre Sutton Manor estate in Hampshire, England. He had land with cattle, a fabulous art collection, and access to people in high places.

He also had three thousand American clients who believed he could make them rich.

The dictionary defines the verb *invest* as "to commit money to earn a financial return," and the verb *gamble* as "to bet on an uncertain outcome." Some people argue they're one and the same. Look at how the banks and Wall Street were behaving in 2008. Others contend that while gambling may be a form of investing, if you are going to succeed as an investor, you need to be a lot smarter than a gambler.

Con men like Alex Herbage who run investment scams always attract their victims by pretending to be smarter than gamblers, and smarter than everyone else, too. So he founded the *IMAC Economic and Financial Review,* the so-called Sutman Institute for Strategic Economic Studies, and the Caprimex Group of companies.

"Maybe you want to gamble," he told potential victims, "but I want to invest."

Herbage studied music as a young man but couldn't make a living conducting and wound up in the record business. When that didn't work, he started a small finance company called Merchant Guaranty Trust. After that business went bust, he opened the Bank of Valette — pretending to have ties to Malta, which he didn't — and offering his customers the possibility of investing in "leading European and British growth stocks." The bank didn't last much longer than any of his other ventures. But a company he'd hidden inside the bank called Eurotrust drew the attention of the police, and he wound up with a six-month jail sentence for violations of the Companies Act.

He followed that with a dance studio that went broke, then headed to the Channel Island of Guernsey where, as an undischarged bankrupt, he opened a financial services business. When the local authorities turned up the heat on Herbage, he left for Zurich where, he claimed, he hooked up with the Greek shipping magnate Stavros Niarchos and began trading commodities.

Around that time, he said, he befriended Bernie Cornfeld, the American ex-pat who'd made a dubious fortune with his fund of funds scheme. Calling himself International Overseas Services, Cornfeld sold investors on his mutual fund that invested in other mutual funds by using the slogan, "Do you sincerely want to be rich?"

Herbage simply took a page out of Cornfeld's playbook and set up a stock exchange for mutual fund clients in Germany. His version of the tale had it that, within a month, he was doing several million dollars' worth of business a day. But then Cornfeld's empire came tumbling down, and Herbage's went the same way.

What Herbage conveniently forgot to add was that the Swiss police raided his Zurich offices and shut him down, leaving debts of $75 million. He also conveniently forgot to say that, over the next four years, another seven companies he'd formed had folded.

Next he started a commodities newsletter. This was long before the days of the Internet, emails, and spam, when financial news-letters were the vogue. They were sent by snail mail — although some were telexed — to paid subscribers who were looking to find a tip or two that could be turned into profits.

"You may want to gamble, but I want to invest," he told his readers and often boasted, "I'm a political economist. I predicted every major move of everything that was happening at that time. The Shah of Persia going, the fall in the pound, the fall in the dollar, and very, very accurately, within two or three cents."

What he was really saying was, this time it could be you.

And people started believing it.

His *Commodities Research Digest* caught on in the United States, and once that happened, the next step was obvious. Instead of picking commodities for others to invest in, he decided that real money could be made inviting his readers to invest with him.

Like all con men working the investment market, he understood that the best way to convince people to hand over their money was to show them how really successful he already was. He established several investment companies in England and Holland, leveraged loans to buy Sutton Manor for just under $1 million, and supposedly sank another half million into it. He told his investors that the house and grounds had been acquired by the Herbage Foundation, a private Swiss charitable trust, whose aims included the development of economic aid to the Third World, medical research, and encouragement of the arts.

With the trappings in place, Herbage ruled Sutton Manor like a feudal lord. Clients who met him there were granted audiences in the throne room. He surrounded himself with a fabulous contemporary art collection, which included outdoor sculptures by Henry Moore, Joan Miró, and Pablo Picasso. He also collected people. His Sutman Institute served the sole purpose of inventing associations with some of England's most respectable names. Pictures of Herbage and British notables frequently appeared in various issues of his *IMAC Economic and Financial Review,* his *Caprimex Group News,* and his *Commodities Research Digest.* There he was alongside former prime minister Edward Heath, shaking hands with the queen's cousin Prince Michael of Kent, posing with the deputy secretary-general of the Commonwealth, discussing matters with leading merchant bankers, and shaking hands with Prince Philip.

To reinforce the myth, he held the Winchester Conference at Sutton Manor, billed as a forum for investment strategies and political freedom. His conferees — mostly subscribers to his newsletters and investors in his funds — were there for the three days and two nights of luncheons, banquets, panel discussions, awards, and excursions to Stonehenge. One afternoon, there was even a medieval jousting match. Herbage used the occasion to announce the winners of the coveted Thomas Paine Awards — which he'd invented — naming former West German chancellor Willy Brandt, U.S. Congressman Ron Paul, and entertainer Danny Kaye as recipients. No one ever bothered to ask if those three knew about this. Herbage simply announced that, unfortunately, they were otherwise busy and unable to attend.

At one point, Herbage maintained a staff of around 140, about one-third of them in his private security force. He claimed to have three offices in England, one in Scotland, one in Amsterdam, a small office in the Cayman Islands and was always just about to open one in Frankfurt.

The heart of his empire was supposed to be Caprimex. He described it as a network of companies through which he serviced investment and financial requirements for clients in ninety-three countries.

In reality, the epicenter of the empire was the morning newspapers, which showed the closing commodity prices from the night before, and a few old computers. Herbage took the papers, sat down at his desk, and invented trades for his clients. They would make a little money one day and lose a little money the next day, but over the course of weeks and months, the nonexistent trades always showed handsome increases in each portfolio's value.

The genie in the bottle — who was pretending to place bets, but only after the race had been run — was making his clients believe that, in a world where amateurs usually lost money, he was an investor, not a gambler, and could annually deliver profits of 30% or more.

His funds were discreetly advertised but heavily subscribed to in the United States. Each client received a monthly statement in a plain envelope. The Cayman Island office, he said, ensured secrecy so that his clients were not subject to any capital gains or other taxes. And, if a client wanted out, he proudly offered cash settlements anywhere in the world.

In other words, if you didn't want anyone

in America to know you were making money on this, Mr. Herbage was promising that whatever he did for you was out of sight of the IRS.

A favorite trick of con men, they love punters who don't want Uncle Sam to know about the money. That's because, if you can't tell the IRS where your money comes from or how much you're making on it, who can you complain to if your money goes walking out the back door?

Had anyone stopped dancing and turned off the music for just a minute they might have spotted the empty bandstand. Herbage was not only spending too much and trying too hard to make people believe that he was, indeed, the best and the brightest genie who could change their luck. He was also particularly clumsy when investors wanted out.

That's a huge footprint in the sand.

As soon as an investor tried to cash out, Herbage had a lame excuse for why he couldn't pay them right away: Wrong address. Our computers are down. My secretary is on holiday. The auditors are working on the accounts. European regulations say I have to wait three business days. When those didn't work, he offered investors extra incentives to stay in. If that didn't work and he was forced to pay out, he paid late. And then, all too often, his checks bounced.

Before long, he simply couldn't get fresh money in fast enough to cover the money that was going out.

Mr. Herbage, meet Misters Ponzi and Madoff.

Just as happened with Van Brink and his alter ego Ira M. Samuels, this genie got stuffed back into the bottle, and it wasn't long before a second genie appeared, offering to clean up the mess made by the first one.

In this case, it was a Finn who lived in the Dutch port city of Rotterdam, and somewhere along the line decided there was a lot of money to be made forming a posse. His partner was an Australian businessman who, at one point, claimed to be an international lawyer, which he was not. Instead, he'd worked for an Italian company, had invested with Herbage, and said he was out of pocket $538,964.88.

The Finn decided the best way to get the Australian's money back — and make a lot more for themselves — was by charging other Herbage victims for the privilege of joining their posse.

After launching a commando-style raid on Sutton Manor, and acquiring a list of Herbage investors plus computer printouts with some Herbage bank accounts, they contacted the three thousand investors and told them that for a down payment of 3.5% of any investor's claim — and a further 6.5% if they succeeded — they would do "whatever is necessary" to seize Herbage's assets.

One of the people who paid for their help was a nervous American man. Call him Clark. He was counting on the Finn and the Australian to recover close to $100,000.

So Clark was now in for an additional $3,500.

Claiming to represent nearly six hundred Herbage investors with interests totaling $15 million — which, at 3.5%, would suggest that the Finn and the Australian had already been paid $525,000 — the Finn said he'd filed a civil action against Herbage and no less than eighteen companies associated with him. A Dutch judge, he went on, had granted their request to freeze five bank accounts in Holland and allow them to seize assets worth around $350 million. Considering that Herbage had gone belly-up for $69 million, the Finn's figures didn't add up.

But Clark, the nervous American investor, was very impressed. Later Clark said he had full faith in the Finn and had no reservations about giving him money. "It's an investment," he said, obviously forgetting the fact that the hundred grand he'd handed over to Herbage was also supposed to be an investment.

The Finn had convincingly assured Clark, "I can change your luck."

What he did for Clark, and whatever other clients he'd managed to lure in, is questionable. The Finn and the Australian did file a few legal actions in Holland, but there is no indication that Clark, or anyone else, ever saw a penny.

Knowing who to trust with your money isn't easy. Be smart and keep these in mind:

- The old expression "never put all your eggs in one basket" holds especially true when investing. With fraudsters ever present in the markets, the question should not be how much can I make? — which is what they want you to think about — but how much can I *lose?*
- Before you hand your money over to someone, even if he has all the trimmings and trappings of success, find out who he really is. It's easy to research someone these days on the net.

Dig as deep as you have to. And be suspicious. Don't look for evidence that he's a con, look for proof positive that he is who he says he is, and honest.

- Any time a trusted person tells you about a great investment opportunity that is available only to a select group of insiders, hold on to your wallet and change the subject.

- If an investment is so good and the payoff is going to be so big, ask yourself, why isn't a bank lending the needed funds? The answer will almost always be because it's much riskier than the sales guy is letting on to or it's an out-and-out scam.

- Beware of flamboyance. There was Ponzi's air-conditioned mansion and heated swimming pool, Madoff's homes and yacht, Herbage's castle and art collection. If the people offering the luscious investment opportunity drive Ferraris, live in mansions, flash fancy watches, flaunt their luxury beach houses, and offer to fly you to your daughter's wedding in their corporate jet — if they make their money by telling you it's an investment when, instead, all they're doing is loading the dice — chances are you've been marked as a potential sucker. It'll be cheaper to buy first-class seats on a commercial flight.

It's one thing to hope a genie will pop out of the bottle. It's another to give him your money.

Chapter Eight:
Maybe This Time
ADVANCE FEE FRAUD

Everybody believes in luck.

We understand that good or bad fortune happens to us by accident or chance, which means it is beyond our control. Flip a coin and the results can be only heads or tails. Now, before flipping the coin, guess on which side it will land. If you've guessed right, you feel lucky. If you've guessed wrong, you feel unlucky. Except you're going to be both lucky and unlucky 50% of the time.

Now, let's say, someone comes along who claims, "I can help you beat the odds. I can help you be right 70% of the time."

As long as the coin and the flip are honest, that's not possible. But what if this person can somehow make you believe that your good fortune is actually within his control? That he can influence your fate? If he can convince you, despite your better instincts, you must just turn a blind eye to the fundamental truth that 50/50 is the only possibility.

That's why, for example, people play the lottery. The odds of winning $40 million are many times more than forty million to one. Yet most of us think, at some time or other, it's worth a buck because "Maybe this time it will be me."

The Ponzis, Madoffs, and Herbages of the world — along with the tens of thousands of others whose names and faces are hidden in the shadows of the World Wide Web — make their living convincing people, "Maybe this time, it will be you."

PAYING UP FRONT

What every con man aims to do is convince you that he can influence the outcome and then take your money before the flip of the coin.

Describing a multitude of sins, advance fee fraud does exactly what it says on the tin — you pay in advance for something that's promised but, in reality, is not going to happen. And it is the single most common category of fraud.

The purest example is the lottery scam. A message comes, either as an email or a phone text, to say you've just won a big prize in some state or national lottery, and all you have to do to collect the money is pay for the handling and postage of the check. The fee can be anything from $35 to $180, it doesn't matter, because whatever you send to the phony lottery redemption office will disappear and you'll never hear from them again.

It's the same with FedEx, UPS, and U.S. Postal Service fraud.

A letter or email that appears to come from FedEx, UPS, or even the USPS says that something valuable is waiting for you at their depot and if you want it delivered you have to pay a small fee. The fact that you're not expecting anything of value and that there is no way to phone anyone to find out what this surprise package of value might be become minor points. Most people are curious. They fall for it because they want to believe.

That's the same reason people fall for ordinary pyramid scams.

THE CHAINS THAT BIND

Nothing more than a chain letter, in the classic pyramid scheme you pay someone for the right to bring more people into the chain who will then pay you for the right to bring more people into the chain who will then pay them, and so forth. And it happens to be illegal.

Not long ago scammers targeted Facebook members — especially college kids — with a pyramid, claiming that this was a way to earn up to one year's tuition. All you had to do was sign up for a website that offered unlimited text chatting. The subscription was $6. You then had the right to invite at least three of your Facebook friends to join, and for each friend who signed up, you'd receive a $2 cut out of their $6 subscription. So, by enlisting only three people, you'd have already made your money back. Better still, the offer continued, for each of your friends who then signed up their friends, you'd receive 25¢.

It's exactly the same rip-off that Louis Gourdain worked with his phony Imperial National Bank endless chain scam all those years ago.

If your three friends enlisted three friends and each of them signed up three more, then nine levels later you'd come out with $7,386. If you could convince six of your friends to sign up six of theirs, and that went on for nine levels, you'd wind up with a whopping $3,023,307.

Sounds great. Except it doesn't work — and can't possibly work. To make that money from the three friends model, you need 29,523 people to play along. In the six friends model, you need 40,310,760 people, which is just over 13% of the entire country.

Yet pyramid schemes abound. And no matter how blue in the face anyone gets trying to explain this one or that one is just a scam, people still fall for them. There are thousands of pyramids and chain letters all over the Internet, and hundreds of them operating as "clubs" throughout the country.

Some promote self-esteem. Others go for the charity angle. Some pretend to celebrate friends and family. Others revolve around "gifts," promoting the totally bogus notion that the money you make is a gift and, therefore, not taxable. But the gimmick is the same — the pyramid.

HOW TO AVOID ADVANCE FEE FRAUD

Avoiding advance fee fraud is easy — don't send anyone any money up front. But there are times when you think you have to. So for those times, consider these points:

1. Know who you're dealing with and where he is.
2. Do not pay a fee on the promise of receiving more money later on.

3. Be absolutely certain you fully understand the deal. Consulting an attorney to keep you out of danger can turn out to be the least expensive part of it.

4. Legitimate businesses have four walls and a roof. They don't operate out of a P.O. Box, and very few use a Hotmail address.

5. Be suspicious of anybody who is asking you for money but is always hiding behind voicemail.

6. Never sign an agreement that impedes you from verifying who you're doing business with. Legitimate people have legitimate references. Con men try to talk you out of them.

In one well-attended support group, eight women join, paying $5,000 each to one woman who is already a member. Each new member recruits eight new members so that she can earn her $40,000. And this is supposed to go on like that forever.

These cons attempt to get around statutes outlawing pyramid scams by claiming to be a multilevel marketing (MLM) operation. They're legal, as long as there is a product on sale somewhere along the chain. But if all you get for your money is the right to recruit new members who then pay you, or you're simply buying the right to sell the product in a certain territory and then sell that right on to someone else, who sells that right to someone else, it's a pyramid, and pyramids are illegal because they're just another example of advance fee fraud.

PLAYING OFF HARD TIMES

The economic downtown of 2008 put pressure on many home owners, who found themselves with property worth less than the mortgage on it. Negative equity and unemployment led to foreclosures, and on the back of that, con men came up with a bunch of new ways to collect advance fees from people who were going broke.

The first was a simple, straightforward con. Claiming to have relationships with the major credit card companies, fraudsters advertised that they could drastically reduce interest rates and minimum payments. Some of them even printed fancy brochures and mailers, with graphs and case histories, just to give the scam a professional financial adviser look. After you filled out a form giving the details of your debt, they returned with a boilerplate paragraph on what they would do and how they would go about doing it. They promised to bring debt down to base and cut minimum payments by two-thirds.

For someone with a credit card bursting

at the limit, this could mean a savings of several thousand dollars. Best of all, they promise, it won't cost you anything because we get our fees by charging the credit card companies for the service.

Huh? The service being, helping the credit card companies make less money? Except there is a sign-on fee of $400. And once you pay it, that's likely to be the last you'll see or hear from them.

A variation on the theme are the agencies that promise to reduce your debt — for a fee — using the legalese double-talk "no money lent" argument. They claim that credit card companies and banks can't collect on the loan because the law states clearly that they cannot legally lend money. So, the argument goes, if they are operating illegally, then the contract binding you to the loan is illegal and, therefore, you don't owe anything. They'll take your case for an up-front fee, which is down to whatever they think they can get out of you. You pay it, and they reassure you, don't worry, the law is the law. But if the law says anything even remotely close to what they claim, that's news to the credit card companies, the banks, their lawyers, and the courts. The problem is, there are loads of websites promoting no money lent scams, and way too many people in serious debt who are willing to grasp at straws as illogical as this.

Some debt elimination scams create fake financial instruments that, in lieu of money, can be used to satisfy credit card companies and the bank. To give them a semblance of legality, these financial instruments come with the Federal Reserve System's seal of approval. Except that the Federal Reserve System does not approve and definitely does not get involved in debt-eliminating programs.

The land patent scam is even less believable. As the number of home foreclosures has risen sharply, con men have poured into the foreclosure-relief market. Several scams have been designed to convince people who are stressed out because they're about to lose their home to sign deeds over on some vague promise of renting now and being able to buy the home back later. That's no advance fee fraud, that's outright theft of someone's home.

The advance fee version is run by people who will argue on your behalf that the bank cannot reclaim your property because it is not in the United States. The fact that these people happen to live in Kansas, Georgia, New Hampshire, Iowa, Missouri, California, or New York is beside the point. For an up-front fee — which can range from several hundred to tens of thousands of dollars — the fraudsters will sell you a land patent that, being legally issued by the U.S. government, designates the land under your property the status of sovereign nation. In return, you are giving up your right to the land. But you still retain title to any buildings constructed on it. If the bank were then to attempt foreclosure, they'd get the house but not the land. Without the land, the house is worthless, so the bank gives up.

Except they don't. You've paid for the fee for this up front and have all the necessary paperwork, and the bank shows up anyway to take possession of your home and the land. You say they can't, their lawyers say they can — and they do. And the fellow who sold you this bill of goods is nowhere to be seen.

Another advance fee fraud invented to separate home owners from their money is the less tax scam. A cold caller knocks on your door and identifies himself as a tax officer from the local town council's property tax office. He's got an ID that looks real and is carrying volumes of property tax records that are real. They are also readily available to anyone who knows how to download them or bothers to go to city hall to fetch them.

He explains there is a property reevaluation under way, and wants you to know that this doesn't necessarily mean that taxes will go up. In fact, he says, that while they generally do their valuations by neighborhood, this year they have started a program by which properties can be individually evaluated. In almost all cases, he goes on, when properties are individually evaluated, taxes go down. Sounds good, you say, sign me up. Unfortunately, he says, there is a fee for that. But then, he reassures you, that the city council has decided that if after an individual evaluation it is decided that the tax must go up, that fee will be refunded. No risk in sight, you hand him your credit card. When he doesn't return a few days later, you phone the property tax evaluation office, and they don't know what you're talking about.

Disappearing middlemen happens all the time with advance fee fraud. So, too, invisible middlemen, like in vehicle matching scams.

You put an ad in the paper to sell your car, and that same day someone gets in touch to say that he's interested. Well, not him exactly but his client. He says, "I'm a private car dealer" — or some sort of middleman — "and my client wants to buy your car." He offers to forward the buyer's details but explains that someone will have to pay his commission. You say, "Let the buyer do it." He says, "Okay, but I don't want the buyer to know." So the two of you conspire to add $250 to the selling price of the car, which the buyer will pay. But because Mr. Middleman needs to be sure that he gets his money, you have to send him the $250 before his client pays you for the car.

Now for the words *vehicle* and *car,* substitute *washing machine, motorcycle, wide-screen TV, boat, old golf clubs, cabin in the woods, eight-track tape collection,* and so on.

Then there is virtual vehicle fraud. (Again, for *vehicle,* substitute whatever else you might be buying.) This time it's you who has spotted an ad for something. You contact the seller, and he's more than happy to negotiate a good price with you. But because the two of you live so far away from each other, the only way he can think of protecting himself — and, at the same time, protecting you — is by using an escrow shipping service. "That way," he explains, "I know you've paid and you know that your money is safe until you receive the item and can see that it's in perfect condition." That sounds okay to you, but you've never heard of escrow shipping services, so he tells you about somethingorotherescrowshipping .com, which he says he's used before. You go to the site, it looks perfectly legit, you fill out all the necessaries, and you pay them. And that's the last you ever see of your money.

PROTECTING YOURSELF

The best way to avoid advance fee scams is never to pay for any goods until you physically take possession of them, and never to pay for services before they're performed.

Also, stay away from:

- Any offer of financial help that you couldn't otherwise get from a lawyer or a legitimate financial institution. Especially if it promises to do what lawyers or legitimate financial institutions can't possibly do, such as automatically repair your credit rating, magically erase your credit card debt, or guarantee a loan or other financing no matter what your situation is. By the way, it is illegal in most states for anyone to promise you a loan and then insist that you pay a commission or fee in advance of signing it.

149

- Anyone who knocks on your door in some sort of official capacity and wants to be paid for whatever service then and there.

CHAPTER NINE:
THE NIGERIAN YAHOO-YAHOO BOYS

Nigerian con men have turned deceit into such a huge industry that it has become a major export and important source of foreign revenue. Celebrated in popular culture as yahoo-yahoo boys — the term probably comes from their use of anonymous yahoo.com email addresses — they are, without any doubt, the biggest international stars in the world of fraud.

Their rise to fame and fortune began in the 1970s, when Nigeria first boomed with oil. A few savvy con men in Lagos understood that they could use the headlines to make money. So they wrote letters, alternately from the National Petroleum Corporation and the Nigerian Central Bank — usually signed by a senior official who had a fancy title like prince — explaining how $45 million was being held overseas and, because of complicated currency laws, they couldn't repatriate the money directly. They went on to say that if you would become their partner and allow them to move the money through your bank account, they would pay you one-third as your commission.

As soon as someone responded favorably — and loads of people fell for it — phone calls and faxes would go to the potential victim to make it all look real and to allay any skepticism. Meetings were even arranged to assure the victim that this deal was on the level.

Money will be wire transferred into your account, they explained, and you should wait until it clears before wiring out our two-thirds.

It all sounded pretty simple. Not to mention a fast way to make $15 million. But then came the kicker — you had to provide the con men with a signed letter to your bank manager, supposedly to authorize the transfer in and then out, but essentially giving the Nigerians paperwork from which they could create a forgery that would then allow them to empty your account. The scam, which was named after the clause in the 1980 Nigerian Criminal Code Act that outlaws it, is forever known as 419 fraud.

In the days of snail mail, it was estimated that 1% to 2% of the people who received a

419 letter fell for it. That might not sound like a lot, but it was believed at the time that the Nigerians were sending out five to ten million of these letters every week. Then, when you understand that the average loss in those days was around $200,000, it's easy to see how it quickly became a multibillion-dollar enterprise.

Today, thanks to email, it is absolutely thriving. Although emails receive fewer hits, sometimes as low as 0.1%, and the average take per hit is way down — usually running in the $5,000 to $50,000 range — emails make it easy to send out hundreds of millions of these scams.

Today, too, they rarely use the Nigerian Central Bank or the National Petroleum Corporation. However, they still sometimes go with the old favorite, Maryam Abacha, who is looking for help to reclaim money that her famously corrupt husband stole from the people of Nigeria. For instance:

Dear Sir
This letter may come to you as a surprise. I am the wife of the late head of state of Nigeria General Sani Abacha, my late husband left huge amount of money in my custody before he died. I am soliciting for your assistance to help me claim fund con-

sealed [*sic*] in three metal boxes deposited in a security company abroad, my main problem now is that the government of my country is sezing [*sic*] all our asset and after us the entire family, what I need from you is to help me claim $20m USD deposited in security company. You are to keep the fund in your account till you and I finalize on how to meet. I intend that if you accept my offer you will be given 30% of the total money after claim.

These fraudsters often take a novel approach. The letters are signed by:

- A lawyer representing a victim of the terrorist attacks on the World Trade Center.
- The operations manager of a bank in Abidjan, Côte d'Ivoire, who found money belonging to a victim of Hurricane Katrina.
- An attractive twenty-five-year-old Sudanese woman living in Senegal who wishes to invest $10.5 million in "your country."
- The head of the "File Department" of the African Development Bank.
- A dying woman who needs you to help her donate her life savings of $15 mil-

lion to charity.

- The young children of a cocoa merchant from Benin who disappeared in France and left $12.6 million, which the French are holding.
- The executive director of the "telex department" of the Bank of Africa in Lomé, Togo, who is looking for help to move $15 million.
- The personal assistant to the director of the "international remittance department" of the Allied and Bond Bank whose poor boss left $30 million after being killed in a plane crash.
- The widow of a man who worked for the "British Judicial Commission" and who is having trouble getting hold of the £10 million he left to her in his will.
- The widow of an assistant to the secretary-general of the Organization of Petroleum Exporting Countries who is looking for help, along with her daughter, in placing $32 million in a shopping mall investment "in your country."
- Joseph Mobutu Sese-Seko, former president of the Democratic Republic of the Congo, who needs your help in his dispute over tens of millions of dol-

lars with the current government, despite the fact that he died in 1997.

There is even a rash of 419 letters that play up America's involvement in Iraq. Several come from U.S. generals who have found Saddam Hussein's hidden fortune and need your help smuggling it out of the country. And this one is a rare gem:

Dear Sir/Madam,
My name is Richard Adams and I am General in US Army and also I was in IRAQ for peace keeping mission.

Before the dead [*sic*] of Saddam Hussein, I went to his house and I saw $19.8 million usd but because of the US Army that is waiting for me outside the house, I gave the money to a Red Cross lady called Mrs. Helen Keyes.

At the moment Mrs. Helen Keyes is in IRELAND with the money and I want you to claim it from her and invest it in your country, because I don't want the Government of America to know about this money.

After you have claim [*sic*] the money, you will collect 30%per [*sic*] from the total amount and invest the remaining 70%per [*sic*] for me in your country. Then I will liveUSA [*sic*] to your country to start a new life there with my family.

Have a nice day. Gen. Richard Adams. (US ARMY)

Poor General Adams plainly skipped too many grammar classes at West Point.

If near-pidgin English isn't clue enough, similar letters are variously addressed to Dearest One, Dear Respectful One, Beloved, Compliments Of The Day To You, Hello Friend, Greetings To You My Dear Friend, Salutations, Dear Partner, and Dear Beloved In Christ.

Spelling mistakes are also rampant.

So it ought to be obvious to anyone receiving one of these that they're scams. But the same way it happens with advance fee frauds, there are people who just want to believe and wind up losing money.

It is not surprising that people who get scammed this way usually complain about it. And so, on the back of those complaints, the Nigerians long ago worked out a second scam to hit the victims again. It's called black money.

The scammer offers to pay you back with a pile of $100 bills that have been overprinted with a special ink. All the money is right there, they say. All you have to do is spring for the expensive chemical it takes to remove the black ink.

As bizarre as it sounds, people fall for this with unsettling regularity. Obviously, the Nigerians set it up elaborately. Men show up disguised as ministers and princes, complete with limos and bodyguards. They are hugely convincing because they know that someone who has been fooled once can be fooled again. They understand that victims of 419 scams are typically so anxious to get their money back that they will indeed hand over more.

In one now famous incident, police intercepted a 419 victim actually on her way to meet some men working a black money scam against her. They explained to her exactly what was going to happen and said that with her help, they could arrest these fraudsters in the act. But she refused to believe them and refused to wear a wire to help them. She arrived at the appointed place only to be told that the venue had suddenly changed — the scammers do that to try to stay one step ahead of the cops — and at the new spot handed over to them a substantial amount of cash.

It was an expensive lesson, because by the time the cops finally caught up with her, the con men were long gone.

A few years ago, the yahoo-yahoo boys

came up with a twist on the twist known as the white money scam. Instead of pieces of paper over-inked in black, these were simply white. The con man said they had been inked white by Americans who'd intended the money to be foreign aid to Sierra Leone. Except they weren't inked at all. And what do white-inked bills have to do with American foreign aid to Sierra Leone? His story was that whenever America shipped money to war-torn parts of the world, they whited out the currency so that the couriers wouldn't steal it. Which doesn't explain how he got it.

"The process to turn the white paper back into one hundred dollar bills," he went on, "required a real bill to be put in between two pieces of white paper, like a sandwich, which would 'magically' turn the white paper into money."

It's comforting to know that all these years later the Nigerians are still coming up with new ideas.

SELLING GREED

While the modern versions of those good old original 419 letters are still bringing income to the yahoo-yahoo boys in Lagos and Abuja, many of these con men have flourished in tough economic times by bombarding America and the rest of the world with offers to help people get out of debt, refinance mortgages, cash in their winning prize, and earn extra money by working at home.

"I'm selling greed," a Nigerian fraudster admitted to Ultrascan, when they did their survey on which people are most susceptible to fraud. "You didn't apply for any lotto, and all of a sudden just see a mail in your mailbox that you're going to win money? That means you have to be greedy."

One of the yahoo-yahoo boys calls himself Macjon, and he has become a very rich man, thanks to a popular work at home scam. Whether his email shows up in your inbox with no warning or you've answered an ad in a free paper, the message is basically the same:

RM FABRICS & TEXTILES Company Ltd
Imports and Exports
General Merchants
Unit 5
Wharram Street, Hull HU2 0JB
Humberside
United Kingdom

Dear Sir/Madam,
Good tidings to you as you read. My name

is Allen Smith of RM FABRICS & TEX-TILES Company Ltd. We have a job offer available for you in which you can earn a lot (weekly). We are an International trading company with our corporate Headquarters based in UK. We deal on raw materials and finished personal care Products including live long products as well as handling of researches.

Due to our competent records we have been receiving orders from NORTHERN AMERICA, AUSTRALIA, and EUROPE which we have not been able to process Competently since we do not have a payment receiving personnel in these Areas. We have decided to recruit payment officers online hence we will be needing a representative to process our payments in these areas.

JOB DESCRIPTION

1. Receive payment from Clients
2. Cash Payments at your Bank
3. Deduct 10% which will be your percentage/pay on Payment Processed.
4. Forward balance after deduction of percentage/pay to any of the offices you will be contacted to send payment To (Western Union Money Transfer).

Mr Allen Smith

To someone looking for a second income, and willing to put in a few hours a week to make 10% of what could be a big sum, this offer sounds very inviting. It also sounds foolproof. After all, what could go wrong?

The answer is, plenty.

The stilted language and phrasing in the letter should be a big clue that this wasn't written by someone whose first language is English. And because it purportedly comes from Great Britain, the less than perfect English should raise alarm bells.

Then, there is no such company called RM Fabrics & Textiles in the UK. Check Google. Check the free online list of incorporated businesses in Great Britain at Company's House in London. It doesn't exist. If that weren't not enough to discourage you from getting involved in this, check Google Maps for the address. In fact, the address is real. There is a Wharram Street in Hull. But when you run the address in Google, what pops up are all sorts of references to other companies, using the same pitch letter, signed by different people.

It's all Macjon, who lives in Lagos, and

personally uses at least nine other aliases through Yahoo!, Virgin.net, BTinternet, and Hotmail. He sends these phony work at home emails from:

- TM Fabrics & Textile International Limited, one of which claims that it's a Latvian textile company. The emails are variously signed by referring agent Harry Collins, Scott Young, Maxwell Carhill, Michael Dixon, Eric Christopher, and Joshua Edwine, whose name also shows up at that address on emails from the Union Food Company Limited.
- Imperial Fabrics, from Jason Brown or Kit Brown.
- Crain Willis & Son Holding Ltd Group, from Maria Jansen or the Reverend Colton Jason.
- Imports and Exports General Merchants, from someone with the odd name Miol Ken.
- Ron White Fabrics Textile International, signed by Ron White, whose name is on the front door but his title is not owner, CEO, or even managing director, but Hiring Coordinator, Human Resources.
- United Asia Trading Company, signed

by Brian White, presumably no relation to Ron, because he's payment manager; David Fisher, who is director of payment, which is not the same job as Brian's; and Bill Swindler, the job instructor with a particularly ironic name.

In all, there seem to be more than three dozen companies using that very same address, with at least as many referring agents. But the satellite view from Google Maps shows Wharram Street as a dead end off to the side of some warehouses. Makes you wonder where all of the referring agents park.

Hedging his bets, just in case you've bothered to check and discovered that the UK companies are shams, Macjon blasts a version of a scam letter using the name of a genuine U.S. company: Hughes Supply in Orlando, Florida, which, of course, has nothing whatsoever to do with this scam. Owned by HDSupply out of Atlanta, a lawyer for the company says the problem came to light in September 2008. They received twenty inquiries about it and have taken up the matter with the Orlando police.

If you swallow Macjon's bait, regardless of whether you're qualified for the job —

how qualified do you have to be to cash a check? — you're automatically hired. Within a week, you receive a check made out to you for $3,200 to $4,800 from a car dealer in Nevada, an oil company in Texas, or, in some cases, the American Bar Association in Chicago. Your instructions are to deposit it in your personal account, wait until it clears, then wire 90% of it to someone designated by Macjon. Bizarrely, that person is always in a third country, such as the Philippines.

Looking at this rationally, none of it makes sense. Why would a foreign company need your bank account to collect funds? Why would Hughes Supply in Orlando need you to collect funds for them in America? Any company with clients in any country can, quite easily and for very little money — certainly much less than 10% — set up a bank account of its own. Or it can put arrangements in place for clients to forward money through another bank. What's more, if a company is operating in the UK, why would it have you send money to the Philippines?

And how come their email addresses don't correspond to the company itself? And how come the phone numbers they list are all cell phones, one of which actually uses an area code in the United Arab Emirates? And how come none of these companies claiming to be at Unit 5, Wharram Street, Hull, Humberside, is listed in the UK phone book?

It doesn't take more than a few minutes of semiclose scrutiny to spot this scam. However, if you flat-out ignore the footprints in the sand, you're in for a real shock. Within a few days of depositing the check, you'll see that the funds are available. So, as instructed, you send 90% to Mr. Smith's pals in the Philippines, and think to yourself, that's the easiest three or four hundred bucks you've ever made.

That is, until a few days after you've wired the money out, when your bank notifies you that the check you deposited was counterfeit. You run to the bank and say, but you guys told me the check cleared. And the bank's answer is "No, we simply made the funds available." It's the same thing, you insist. And the bank says, "No, sorry, the check did not clear; we advanced the money to you as a service — most banks do this for their clients — the check was bogus, we're withdrawing the money, and the funds you've already used is what you now owe us."

Investigators in Britain who have tracked

Macjon say that during November and December 2008, he targeted 13.5 million Americans with that email. They estimate his success rate at around 0.1%. That's 13,500 victims. While reported losses go from $3,000 up to a whopping $200,000, if you just take the low end, it means that Macjon stole $40.5 million in less than two months.

AN HONEST-TO-GOD TRUE ENCOUNTER

Meet Macjon wannabe and yahoo-yahoo barrister, Regan Miller. That's his genuine phony name, although he's almost certainly not a barrister.

According to his email, he's just been authorized to send his potential victim (PV) $250,000. And all the PV has to do is use Western Union to wire him $180 to cover the wire fee. He's included a phone number in his email, so the PV — feeling mischievous — calls him from New York. Unfortunately for Barrister Regan, it's the middle of the night in Abuja, Nigeria.

He answers the call half asleep.

The PV asks, "Is this Mr. Miller?"

He hesitates, as if he can't remember all the aliases he uses. "Ah . . . yes?"

There is a brief discussion about who's

calling him — "It's because I got an email that says I've won the lottery" — and at first Regan seems suspicious. He wants to know when the email was received. That's probably because he can't recall which scam he used this time.

"Must have been a while ago," the PV says, "because it's been sitting in my inbox. I've been away and I only just got back. Gee, I hope it isn't too late. It does say that I needed to respond within three days. I'm real sorry."

"Listen carefully," he says. "The amount has been temporarily withdrawn for lack of being able to make the payment on time. So it is impossible for you to pick your winnings up from the Western Union location. Without a response from you, it was withdrawn for security reasons."

"I understand but" — here come the elephant tears — "please don't tell me I lost all this money. Please don't tell me it's gone."

It's not that Regan has a soft spot. "No, no, you haven't. You really haven't." It's that he thinks he's landed a sucker. "You need to follow the instructions. Pay for the charges of one hundred eighty dollars and once your payment has been confirmed, then ten thousand dollars will be paid to you now. The rest will come later."

"Wow, that's great. Really. But tell me, why can't you just take it out of the ten grand? You know, send me ten grand minus the one eighty?"

He's heard that one before and he's ready for it. "Because the fee is for Western Union and they need to be paid. Anyway, the law won't allow this."

"Well, we wouldn't want to break the law."

"Not a problem at all," he says. "If there is a problem it is probably at your end. So you have to do what is necessary and then we will send you ten thousand dollars within twenty-four hours."

It has to go to a specific person at Western Union in Nigeria. The yahoo-yahoo boys use Western Union because they're franchises; each store is managed locally so on-the-ground controls can be very weak. They can receive money with nothing more than a reference number and a phony ID. They have even started obtaining Western Union franchises to make it easier still for themselves and more difficult for investigators.

"Once he receives the money from you," Regan goes on, "he will be able to send you the ten thousand dollars right away and then you will receive all two hundred and fifty thousand dollars, just like the letter says. So go ahead and send the payment to him."

"Oh . . . okay. But, does he know that I'm late? Because this says respond in three days . . ."

"It's been a week, if I'm not mistaken . . ." Actually, it was more than a month, but we won't let minor details get in the way. "So I'm advising you what's best."

"Are you sure that it will be all right?"

He's starting to get a little annoyed with all these questions, especially at this hour of the night, and changes tack to insist that there is an immediacy to this. "I need to ask you some questions. Because I have received a notice from the compensation committee to withdraw this. So I would like to know, how soon are you going to make the payment so you can start receiving the benefit?"

No reason to let him get back to sleep too soon. The PV wants to know, "How's first thing in the morning? That all right?"

Hardly. "I think you're very lucky. But my advice is if you have the funds today you should do it today. Listen to the implications. Over here, there is a big time difference between Nigeria and America, so if you send the payment today, then it will be here tomorrow."

Now comes another question he's certainly heard before. "Oh . . . ah . . . just one more thing. How did I win this lottery? Because I don't remember ever applying for it."

He's got to be asking himself, why won't this character just send the money and let me get back to bed? "Listen carefully," he says, and somehow gets his scams slightly confused. Who knows how many others he's running? "It isn't a lottery. What is actually going on is the federal government compensation policy. The government of Nigeria is compensating individuals from your country, the United States of America, due to a monetary request from the United Nations."

Three cheers for the good old UN. "Why are they doing that?"

"They're asking the Republic of Nigeria to compensate those living in other countries."

What nice people. "So it's not a lottery?"

"It's just a compensation from the federal government. It's simple, okay?"

Sure it is. "Kind of like Santa Claus, huh?"

He's obviously too tired to find that funny. "Just send the money."

DOING BUSINESS IN YAHOO-YAHOO LAND

The yahoo-yahoo boys have made legitimate business with West Africa almost impossible. By raping their national patrimony, they have cast suspicion on all business communication from Nigeria. It's difficult to know who to trust. Obviously, there are legitimate people throughout Nigeria who do business — or try to, or hope to — with Americans. But credibility is not a Nigerian businessman's strong suit. The yahoo-yahoo boys have managed to throw any semblance of that out the window.

Simply put, you should not believe, and therefore quickly disregard, any unsolicited email that has anything at all to do with West Africa — not just Nigeria — because a few years ago the yahoo-yahoo boys got smart, understood that the word *Nigeria* in an email is a huge red flag, and ever since have tried to pretend that they're writing from other countries. But the scam is the same.

On the other hand, if you are contacted by a company that seems legitimate and has a legitimate-sounding offer addressed directly to you or your business by name, you can protect yourself by thinking first and foremost about your downside.

Always assume the possibility of a swindle and put the burden of legitimacy squarely on the other side.

Legitimate West African companies with a track record of honest business have just that, a track record. Legitimate companies or legitimate businesspeople who don't yet have a track record should be anxious to build one. And there are plenty of ways to demonstrate legitimacy:

- Start with the U.S. Commercial Service Office, located at the U.S. Consulate in Lagos, Nigeria (www.buyusa .gov/nigeria/en). They offer a wide array of services to help anyone planning on doing business with Nigerians and especially help in determining whether the people you're intending to do business with are genuine. The office provides research and can also put you in touch with businesses and businesspeople who *prequalified*, which means registered with them, and have been vetted to some extent by the consul's officers on the ground. A commercial specialist from the office can also investigate a company on your behalf by checking a physical location, business licenses, and contacts to determine legitimacy. This first step alone should weed out the majority of fraudsters who pop up in so many financial transactions having to do with Nigeria.

- Have your prospective business partners submit an international company profile, such as a Dunn & Bradstreet report. Be wary of any business that cannot provide such a report, or of any that have been listed within the past few days.
- Seek references. Legitimate companies have legitimate references. Suspect businesspeople have suspect references or none at all. Legitimate companies will happily provide them. Suspect businesspeople will do their damnedest to talk you out of them.
- Arrange for any payments to be made through an American law firm, which will hold money wired to them through the legitimate banking system in escrow, until goods and services are delivered.

Legitimate businesspeople may find this tiresome, but if they want to do business, they will agree to your conditions. Fraudsters will tell you this is insulting, argue and cajole, then cancel the deal and move on to find another potential victim. For Americans looking to do business with Nigeria, it's a win–win.

CHAPTER TEN:
SNAKE OIL

Snake oil salesmen have been conning the public ever since the public decided that maybe, just maybe, this horrible-tasting stuff works.

One of America's legendary hucksters was William Avery Rockefeller (1810–1906), the father of John D. Rockefeller, these days remembered as the richest man the world has ever seen. But long before the surname became synonymous with oil, banks, real estate, and politics, the patriarch of the family was calling himself "Doctor William Rockefeller, the Celebrated Cancer Specialist," and traveling the country selling herbal remedies. He'd buy a barrel of a laxative made with petroleum for $2, pour it into a thousand six-ounce bottles, and call this magic potion Nujol. His pitch was that Nujol cured all forms of cancer that had not already become terminal. He was a womanizer and bigamist, and after being accused of fraud, horse thievery, burglary, arson, counterfeiting, and rape, he changed his name to "The Celebrated Dr. William Levingston" and kept right on selling false hopes. He was so good at it that he sold each six-ounce bottle for $25, which was then around two months' pay for the average workingman.

Today, the snake oil business is much the same, except that false hopes are no longer flogged off the back of a buckwagon. Instead, we have the Internet and cable TV.

The snake oil industry flourishes in spite of the efforts of the Food and Drug Administration (FDA) to corral all this phony stuff with regulations and programs aimed at educating the public. Among the many most popular and insidious cons are:

- **Arthritis Fraud.** According to the government, arthritis affects nearly 15% of the population, which represents a huge potential market. Making it especially attractive to con men is the fact that more than nine out of every ten sufferers buys some form of self-treatment. Whether or not they see a doctor, they are still willing to pay for copper ionized bracelets, vitamins, herbal potions, exotic balms, insect extract concoctions, and even snake venom. Although there is an argument to be made about the positive effect that mere belief in a treatment can have, the FDA insists that most, if not all, of these things do not work.

- **Miracle Breakthrough Treatments for Frightening Horrible Diseases Fraud.** It would be cruel to blame anyone stricken with a serious illness for trying anything and everything to survive. It is even crueler for fraudsters to promise a cure that doesn't work, especially because so many people who opt in to these miracle breakthroughs then opt out of sound medical advice and treatments. Unfortunately, the Internet is overloaded with miracle breakthroughs, charlatans, and clinics in the Caribbean, the Orient, and Latin America — especially Mexico — that are blatant frauds. Their miracle breakthroughs, which come with hefty price tags, are all unproven and mostly useless. Distilled fruit seeds will not cure cancer. Volcanic ash mixed with algae and South American jungle tree bark will not restore youth. Consider the fact that, if any miracle breakthrough offered even a glimmer of hope, it could be worth tens of billions to major pharmaceutical companies. With that kind of money in the game, the global players would be onto it in a heartbeat, dispatching armies of scientists and lawyers to grab patents, secure FDA approval, and push it onto the market.

- **Weight Loss Fraud.** Whether it's a skin patch, grapefruit pills, or capsules filled with exotic Chinese herbs, they're only about hope and not about anything that is going to get you slim.
- **Discount Fraud.** A crooked telemarketing company in Canada advertised cut-rate drugs to American seniors, and added free benefits for the purchase of a loyalty program card. To sign up, seniors were asked about bank account and credit card numbers. The company then charged $399 to the seniors' bank or credit card, as a onetime fee for the loyalty card, which turned out to be useless.
- **Size and Libido Fraud.** Sold over the Internet and under the counter, anything that promises to increase male genitalia size, female breast size, permanently cure impotence, or turn you into a superstud is a scam. They

don't work and won't work, but they can pose serious health risks.

PRESCRIPTION DRUG FRAUD

Perhaps the most dangerous scam of all, prescription drug fraud turns on counterfeit medicines — and they can be lethal.

By definition, a counterfeit medicine is one that contains the wrong active ingredients, is made with the wrong amount of ingredients, contains no active ingredients, is somehow contaminated, and/or comes in phony packaging. Because of the way the pharmaceutical companies run their marketing businesses and price their drugs and because so many seniors are on fixed incomes — some of whom are actually forced to choose between medicine and food — it is understandable that when they hear about cheap prescription drugs available on the Internet, by mail, or over the phone, they're interested. But there are two very specific dangers to consider when it comes to cheap prescription medicines. First, you don't always know who you're buying from. And, second, you don't necessarily know *what* you're buying.

In some cases, these scams are easy to spot. For example, beware of sites that advertise cheap meds where "no prescription is necessary" and "our doctors will write the prescription for you." By definition, the service they are offering is illegal. In practice, they're frauds.

To begin with, prescribed drugs cannot be obtained without a prescription. While sellers may advertise that their doctor will supply the prescription, even if that were legal, it would still be absolutely crazy. The American Medical Association insists that if you accept a prescription from a doctor who has not first given you a physical exam, the drugs prescribed might be, at best, inappropriate and, at worst, downright dangerous.

You also need to be wary of sites selling prescription medicines that do not list an address and phone number, or where a phone number is listed but doesn't correspond to the address. There are thousands of them.

Some online med sites sell only lifestyle *drugs,* such as those that treat obesity, sex drive, and hair loss. Some specialize in miracle or breakthrough drugs for arthritis, osteoporosis, and a long list of other diseases, especially cancer and AIDS. Some sell products that they insist can be used to treat a variety of serious but otherwise unrelated conditions. Or they sell drugs on the back of wild promises of greatly increased cognitive function. Or they market drugs with no side effects. Or they advertise products that "make doctors' visits no longer necessary."

They're scams.

The sites are run by con men operating out of Mexico, Thailand, China, Africa, the subcontinent, and eastern Europe. They sell you unidentified pills in a plastic bag or counterfeit pills in counterfeit packaging or just charge your credit card and never bother sending you anything.

ONLINE PHARMACIES

A caveat also comes when dealing with online pharmacies, especially those in Canada.

Because of the way the Canadian government buys medicine for their national health service, U.S.-manufactured prescription drugs can be sold in legitimate Canadian pharmacies for 30% to 50% less than the exact same drug in the United States. Seniors cottoned on to this years ago, and in response to them, legitimate Canadian pharmacies have a big presence on the Internet. But then, so do the fraudsters pretending to be Canadian pharmacies.

One so-called Canadian pharmacy, for example, offers highly discounted medicines and displays phone numbers in New York and London. But they have a postal address in Cyprus. When you search for their IP address, you find the website operating in Odessa, Ukraine, and the registered owner of it using an address in Minsk, Belarus.

Dialing the 800 number at around 9:00 p.m. gets you a young man who answers the phone with a heavy Russian accent. He's asked where he is in Canada. He answers that he is working at the Canadian pharmacy's call center in London, England. Which means, for him, it's the middle of the night. How many legitimate Canadian pharmacies have call centers in Britain? The answer is, absolutely none. Why would they? And how come this guy is still there at 2:00 a.m.?

He confirms what it says on the website, that no prescriptions are necessary for any of the drugs listed, and, yes, he says, they feature big discounts on brand-name drugs. One of them is Cialis, manufactured by Eli Lilly to compete with Pfizer's Viagra. Bought via prescription in the United States, Cialis should cost around $10 a pill. Lilly insists that there is no such thing as generic Cialis, and advises that anyone who finds the drug sold on the Internet for, say, $3 a pill is not getting Cialis. They caution that the active ingredient in the $3 version may be different, the stated dose may be wrong, and the manufacturing of the pill — even if it says Cialis on it — is highly questionable.

They emphatically warn, whatever it is, you should not be taking it.

But the Canadian-New York-London-Cyprus-Ukraine-Belarus pharmacy is selling pills clearly marked Cialis for $1.01 each.

It's real, the fellow with the Russian accent insists. He even points to the website's full page of testimonials that praise their products: "Your pills are fantastic. I have observed no any [*sic*] side effects."

"Sounds like they're fine," the caller comments.

"They are," he says. "The quality of the pills we're selling are really good. They're all Indian FDA approved. And we have been in business for fifty years."

The Indian FDA? They do exist. But how reliable they are, by North American standards, how well they oversee the Indian drug market, and just how safe and effective the Indian drug market is are all fair questions. The American FDA is skeptical enough to have opened two of its own offices in India. Consumer caution seems justified.

As for the fifty-year-old Canadian pharmacy claim, if that were true, you would think they'd have established their website long before their official registration date — November 2005.

CHEAP MEDS FROM CANADA

In an effort to clarify what is, clearly, a murky situation, the FDA took to the web not long ago, looking at Canadian pharmacies offering cheap meds to Americans. They discovered no fewer than eleven thousand websites. A Google search of the term *Canadian pharmacy* returns 3.6 million hits. But, according to the FDA, there are only 214 licensed pharmacies in Canada that sell over the Internet.

Those other Canadian pharmacy sites are, exactly like the one out of Ukraine, businesses pretending to be in Canada but that are actually in Pakistan, Thailand, Vietnam, Mexico, Cyprus, the Caribbean, and throughout the former USSR. The FDA even found one so-called Canadian pharmacy located in Washington State.

Pharmaceutical manufacturers in the United States are constantly trying to warn seniors that they shouldn't be buying drugs online from anywhere, including Canada, because the drugs may not be safe. This despite the fact that many of the drugs sold by legitimate Canadian pharmacies are manufactured in the United States by those same U.S. companies.

The fifteen major drug wholesalers in Canada are permitted to buy drugs from manufacturers anywhere in the world. So the FDA does have a point, because it's not necessarily always true that U.S.-branded drugs come from the United States. Therefore, fearing that manufacturing standards beyond their jurisdiction may not be acceptable, the FDA's position is that virtually all shipments of prescription drugs imported from outside the country — which includes drugs bought online from a legitimate Canadian pharmacy — violate the law. And to some extent, they have cracked down. U.S. Immigration and Customs Enforcement (ICE) agents work alongside U.S. postal inspectors to intercept drugs coming into the country from Canada. Although Canadian pharmacies report that around 98% of their shipments get through.

The U.S. government has also, at times, put pressure on Visa and MasterCard to stop payments for these Internet purchases, while the FDA has threatened legal action against insurance companies that cover sales from Canada. In a few rare instances, federal agents have actually boarded buses with seniors returning from day trips to Canada to inspect the medications they bought there.

As annoying as it might be to think that Washington has been stopping drug importation because the Big Pharma lobby is protecting their price monopolies in Congress, the phony medicine industry does pose a genuine problem. It's estimated to be worth in excess of $75 billion a year, and the immediate health dangers posed by pills manufactured and/or sold by unknown sources is just as enormous. So, again, yes, to some extent the FDA does have a case.

A few years ago, a drug counterfeiter in Africa sold a huge shipment of phony birth control pills to a Brazilian distributor, with predictable results. More recently, counterfeit medicines coming out of China were responsible for several hundred deaths. The World Health Organization estimates as many as one in four drugs sold in the developing world are counterfeit. When criminals counterfeited Procrit, which is used by cancer patients for fatigue and anemia, they used nonsterile tap water and in the wrong proportion, creating a serious risk of infection for the patients who were depending on those pills to stay alive.

Around the same time, a shipment of two hundred thousand counterfeit Lipitor tablets, a drug used to reduce cholesterol, was seized. No one knows how many more of those counterfeit Lipitor pills made their way onto the market. In other cases, deaths have resulted in men with heart conditions taking counterfeit Viagra.

A criminal drug gang recently busted in Great Britain was selling counterfeit anti-malarial pills that contained traces of sildenafil, the main ingredient in Viagra. They were also selling fake Viagra, Cialis, and Propecia. It is worrying that the bunch turned out to be the local distribution arm of an organized criminal enterprise operating out of China, with ties to India and Pakistan and distribution networks throughout the Caribbean and in the United States.

But none of those case studies means that seniors who can find genuine prescription drugs from genuine pharmacies in Canada shouldn't be permitted to buy them.

On the other hand, those case studies do prove that anyone who swallows a pill when he doesn't know what the pill is or where it came from is taking unacceptable risks.

You can, however, work around those risks. It just takes time and effort.

If you're looking to buy meds from an online pharmacy in North America, you need to make certain that the site is a legitimate pharmacy. In the United States, check with the National Association of Boards of Pharmacy (www.nabp.net) or by phone, 847-391-4406. If you're shopping for prescription medicine from Canada, each province has a pharmaceutical board that can provide information. There is also the Canadian International Pharmacy Association (www.ciparx.ca), which governs and upholds the ethical and professional practice of international pharmacies. Their number is 204-453-6586.

And then there is pharmacychecker.com, a site that independently checks the credentials of online pharmacies in the United States and Canada and publishes drug price comparison charts.

It is important to restate that *legitimate pharmacies have legitimate addresses and legitimate phone numbers.* Unlike that website in the Ukraine, pretending to be in Canada, legitimate pharmacies have four walls and a roof. They have an address and a phone number that corresponds to that address. They don't have a Toronto postal code and a Mexican area code. They have licenses, will sell only on a prescription that you must supply, and have a licensed pharmacist on duty to answer questions. Canadian prices will usually be lower than U.S. prices, but they won't be bargain-basement lower. If you find sites with lots of product promotions, enormous discounts, and all sorts of special deals, be skeptical.

Real pharmacies don't just sell lifestyle drugs or miracle breakthroughs for serious diseases or products that treat several serious but otherwise unrelated illnesses. Fraudsters do that.

When meds bought online arrive, it is vitally important to check the packaging very carefully. It can be difficult to tell a counterfeit pill from the real thing at first glance, so you need to look at lot numbers and at the pills themselves. You need to compare everything with the same meds in a local pharmacy. Check size, shape, and color and, eventually, be aware of the taste. Never take any medicines from an unsealed container. If in doubt, consult a pharmacist or a physician.

If, after taking a pill bought online, you suffer any change or sudden reaction to it, consult your physician immediately.

Finally, if you believe you have bought a counterfeit drug, you can save other people from serious harm by reporting it to the

FDA's Medwatch program (www.fda.gov/medwatch) or by phone, 800-332-1088.

CHAPTER ELEVEN:
DEFRAUDING SENIORS

The call that morning went like this:

"Grandma, it's me." The boy was crying. "Help. I'm in trouble."

"What's wrong?" the woman demanded excitedly, just assuming that it was her grandson. After all, who else called her "Grandma"?

"I got arrested in Canada." He barely managed to explain through his tears, "For illegal fishing. It's dumb. We were fishing without a license. No one told us we needed a license. But the cops didn't want to know. Please help. I'm in jail. I have to pay forty-two hundred dollars. It's six hundred as a fee and thirty-six hundred for bail. Otherwise they're going to keep me in jail for weeks. Please, help me, Grandma . . ."

She reassured him, "Of course I will." She promised, "I'll do whatever you want me to."

He gave her the payment instructions — a

name and an address for a MoneyGram —
warned that the whole amount had to be
wired that morning, kept saying thank you
and I love you, and assured her that he'd
phone again as soon as he got out of jail.

Clearly upset by this phone call, her
anguish and his sense of urgency clouded
her thinking. She rushed to the bank and
made arrangements to wire $4,200 to
Canada. Only later did she wonder, why
didn't he call his parents? And how come
his voice sounded older? And why would he
be fishing in Canada when he's supposed to
be in school a thousand miles away?

Seniors are especially vulnerable to fraud in
two very specific areas. The first is money
matters, such as investments, banking, and
insurance. The second is health.

Without trying to be too cute, here's one
way of looking at how con men approach
seniors. The process is called GIPP, as if it
were pronounced "gyp."

Step 1: Give the senior something he or
she wants or thinks that he or she needs
and doesn't already have: financial security, a low-interest loan, antiaging creams,
deep-discount pharmaceuticals, a new car,
a trip, a way to protect loved ones.

Step 2: Immediacy creates confusion: You must act immediately; this is a onetime offer that is going to expire in the next few minutes; you have to tell me right now, yes or no, because if you say no, I have to offer it to someone else right away; the discount is good only if you pay by credit card or bank transfer right now, otherwise you'll have to pay the full price.

Step 3: Pretend to help solve the confusion: I'm calling back again, even though you asked me not to, because I went to my boss and he said he would extend the special price offer; I cannot send you anything in writing before you agree, but as soon as you do I will courier over to you everything you need to have; I'm doing this for you because I would hope that, if my parents were in the same situation, someone would be nice to them.

Step 4: Pry loose your prize: We're an old, well-established company. Just ask anyone. But I don't want you to lose out on this, so just trust me. You can hear from my voice that I'm trying to help. Let me have your credit card; I promise you, it's absolutely free, although there is a minor fee for postage and handling, but don't worry about that, it's standard stuff, and anyway, the credit card helps us verify your address.

There are several reasons why con men single out seniors.

To begin with, they have money. Even if many seniors are living on a fixed income, generally speaking as a group, they have cash in the bank. Many own their own homes, and their property is often mortgage free. Many also have credit cards with above-average spending and cash-advance limits because they tend to pay their balances in full every month.

Then, the older we get, the less capable we tend to be when it comes to handling stressful and confusing situations.

Crooks also see seniors as a low-risk target, being less likely than other groups to report fraud. Some senior victims are too embarrassed about having been taken. Some don't want their sons or daughters to think that they're no longer capable of handling their own finances. Others don't know how to go about reporting a crime and worry that, if they do, there could be ramifications. And then, if they do choose to fight back, they often make poor witnesses. Memory isn't what it used to be. Exact dates and times are difficult to recall.

Verbatim conversations and precise descriptions get muddled.

Con men only have to worry about a trial if they actually get arrested. And the odds of that happening are remote because they build safeguards into their scams. The most important precaution they take is to put state lines and international borders between themselves and their victims. Why take a big risk by running a scam down the block, when the Internet, phones, faxes, credit cards, and online bank transfers make it so simple to sit, comfortably and anonymously, hundreds if not thousands of miles away?

In the case of the panicky call to the grandmother for $4,200, she got lucky. Someone at her bank saw money being wired to Canada and routinely notified their fraud department. As Florida's seniors have been plagued with calls pretending to be grandchildren in distress — flooding the state attorney general's office with complaints — warnings have gone out through the local media that if you're asked to wire money to Canada, that could be a red flag to fraud.

The bank took the trouble to ask her if this was what she really wanted to do. But if they hadn't, then what? Say she reported the crime to the police. All they'd have to go on is a name and an address at the end of a wire transfer. It's obvious that the chance of finding anyone so far away, or of recouping the victim's money, is pretty remote. But say the local cops did take the trouble to notify their counterparts in Canada. Then what? Most likely nothing because whoever fetched the money would have used a phony name.

But let's say that the Canadian police did get lucky and tracked down the swindler, arrested him, and put him on trial. Then what? They'd notify the victim in Florida that she's expected to come to Canada to testify. And the chances of that happening? Between airfare, hotel and food costs, the time spent waiting to go in front of a jury, and all the stress, it's not surprising that many victims either can't afford or can't be bothered to do that.

With the odds heavily weighted in the con man's favor, especially those who work the lucrative seniors' market, is it any surprise that they have every incentive to keep on offending?

TELEPHONE MARKETING
When the Federal Trade Commission conducted a recent survey on fraud, they found

that more than twenty-five million adults in the United States fall victim each year. Out of that, around $40 billion is stolen annually from seniors, and those figures are increasing.

Because the telephone is the easiest way to reach seniors — nearly a third of all telemarketing fraud victims are age sixty or older — it's estimated that there are fourteen thousand illegal telemarketing gangs burning up phone lines every day, trawling for victims. Telephone fraud offers con men a huge directory of potential victims — the phone book. It's cheap and easy, guarantees a psychological distance between himself and his potential victims, and provides easy ways to hide.

Some seniors are targeted relentlessly, receiving twenty or more calls a day from con artists. Either their name is on a list of people who have been bilked before — fraudsters sell lists of victims to each other — or con men are phoning back again and again just to wear the person down. Unfortunately, if you have been victimized once, you can expect to be targeted again. Calls may even come from "Good Samaritans" who will commiserate with you, then offer to help you get your money back. But that's a scam, too.

For many seniors, distinguishing between an honest telesales agent and a thief is not easy. Obviously, there's no way to tell how honest someone is by the tone of their voice — that's why it's called "sweet talking" — but many seniors just don't want to believe that the pleasant-sounding young man or woman on the other end of the phone could possibly be trying to steal their money.

At the same time, they may believe that hanging up on that person is rude. All the more so when the person is offering something that sounds worthwhile — a prize; a huge discount; a subscription; a vacation; insurance; cheap meds; low-cost vitamins; health care; a once-in-a-lifetime, strike-it-rich, can't-miss investment; even kinship and romance.

Taking advantage of very cheap telecommunications, gangs of con men staff boiler rooms throughout the world, calling seniors in the United States with a carefully scripted spiel, pretending to be stock brokers with hot shares to sell. The shares may be real, but the companies behind them are on life support or are already clinically dead; or the fraudsters are purposely pumping up the prices of the shares so that they can dump them at the top of the market and leave everyone else hanging on to the wreckage; or the shares are totally fraudulent because the companies don't exist. These boiler-room operations have mastered high-pressure techniques and ruthlessly consider seniors to be sitting ducks.

Given the fact that the bad guys are so very good at being bad guys — and have absolutely no qualms or conscience when it comes to irreparably harming people who cannot always defend themselves — the first thing seniors need to learn is how to hang up.

After all, the same people who spent years as young parents warning their children, "Never talk to strangers," are now taking phone calls from total strangers, buying stuff from them that they don't need or can't afford, or handing out valuable information — credit card numbers, bank details, Social Security number, driver's license number, mother's maiden name, Medicare number — as if they'd known the person on the other end of the line forever.

They would never answer the same questions if a stranger came up to them on the street, and yet so many of them spend time on the phone doing just that.

Seniors need to know:

- Telemarketers, even honest ones, are not your friends.
- Just because someone sounds pleasant, it doesn't mean he's honest.
- Fraudsters pressure people into buying something immediately or sending money immediately. They will warn you, act right now or the offer goes away. Legitimate companies don't do that.
- If you ask a legitimate company making a legitimate telesales pitch to send you written information, they will do that. If the caller won't, or tries to talk you out of it, there's something wrong.
- If you tell a legitimate telesales person that you're not interested, he should go away. If you say you want to check it out and get back to him, he should give you a name and number to call. If the person phoning won't do either, just hang up.

Then, seniors also need to be especially suspect of anyone on the phone who says:

- "You've won this great prize." Unless you entered the contest, don't believe it. They may say, it's a phone company contest to promote use of the telephone. Or it's Microsoft promoting use of the Internet. Not true. Because after the fellow phoning you gets you excited about the prize, he'll tell you that you have to pay for postage, handling, tax, or other charges. It's a scam. It's also illegal in most states for anyone holding a contest or a sweepstakes to require payment to claim a prize.

- "We will send our representative, or a courier, to pick up your check." Don't allow that. He's either trying to get inside your front door, or looking for cash so that there won't be any way to trace the con back to him.
- "No need to speak to anyone else about this, or get written confirmation, because this is totally on the level." People who say that aren't.

To protect yourself, the most basic rules apply:

- Always demand to know who you're talking to. Legitimate salespeople will give you their name, a contact number, their business address, and sometimes even a company ID number. Fraudsters will try to talk you out of that, talk around it, or give you false information.

- Never give any personal information, whatsoever, to anyone over the phone, no matter who he says he is or where he's phoning from. If the person insists he's legitimate and that this is important, tell him to write to you, but don't give him your name or address. After all, if it is legitimate and he already has your number, then he knows who you are and where you can be reached.

- Don't buy anything, invest in anything, or make any donation to charity without having everything spelled out first in writing. And then don't automatically believe that just because it's written down it's true.

- Do not pay for services in advance. However, if you are buying a product, you need to make certain that you will receive what you're paying for. And you can't just take the seller's word for it.

AVOIDING THE TELEMARKETERS

You can further protect yourself, at least to some extent, from the nuisance of telemarketers and prerecorded sales pitches by enrolling in the National Do Not Call

Registry. Once you're on the list, legitimate telemarketers are not supposed to call. Whoever does should then be considered suspect, and you can report them. But you'll need to keep a record of names and dates of those calls.

Using the phone you want to register, call 888-382-1222 (TTY: 866-290-4326) or do it online (www.donotcall.gov). Registration is free and lasts five years, after which time you will have to reregister. If you change your number, you will also need to reregister. It's not a perfect system, because nonprofit groups, charities, political organizations, and survey companies are not required to check with the registry before calling. However, in many of those cases, if you ask that they not phone you again, they should take your number off their list.

At the same time, relatives and friends need to recognize some of the footprints in the sand that will inevitably show up if a senior has gotten into trouble. Be on the lookout for:

- Tons of junk mail for trips, prizes, and sweepstakes.
- Frequent calls from strangers offering great moneymaking opportunities, investments, stock tips, or to collect

money already lost to telemarketers.

- Payments to out-of-state companies or payments to obscure companies in other countries.
- Suspicious payments that are being picked up by courier services.
- Lots of cheap prizes that are suddenly arriving, like costume jewelry, small appliances, beauty products, and water filters.

If any of these things are evident, it could be that a fraudster has already struck.

CHECK FRAUD

Because seniors are less likely to do their banking online, they are more prone to check fraud. It's a low-tech crime but one that cannot be ignored.

It frequently begins with lost or stolen checks. And if a check goes missing, it should be reported to the bank immediately. Same if you've ordered new checks or deposit slips, and they haven't been delivered in a reasonable amount of time. Notify your bank.

You also need to pay attention to ATM receipts. They may contain more information about your bank account than you want strangers to know. Take the receipt home and, if you're not going to save it, shred it.

When you order new checks, print only your first initial with your name on them — J. Smith. Then, when you use those checks, sign your full name — John Smith. The idea is that if you lose a check, whoever finds it and tries to use it will sign J. Smith and that should be a signal to your bank that you didn't sign it.

Finally, buy your checks only from established vendors. Be suspicious of discounted offers in emails or junk mail. (Also see "Check Fraud" on page 244.)

Additional scams aimed at seniors include:

- **Reverse Mortgage.** Sometimes known as Home Equity Conversion Mortgages (HECMs), these mortgages were created to give an opportunity to seniors to supplement their income by taking equity out of their homes. You can take the money as a lump sum, in monthly payments, or as a line of credit. The loan carries interest and gets repaid when the borrower dies, moves, or sells the property. Legitimate HECMs are insured by the Federal Housing Authority (FHA). However, unscrupulous real estate professionals, home financial advisers, loan officers, appraisers, developers, and builders — who frequently use church groups and other affinity opportunities to make contact — have been bringing seniors into this scam, knowingly or otherwise, and exposing them to financial losses and legal repercussions. The fraudster buys a property — often one that has just been repossessed or one that is derelict — then transfers the deed to you, sometimes with money changing hands. You must live in the place for at least sixty days in order to declare the property your primary residence. A false appraisal is arranged, inflating the value of the property, at which point you are instructed to apply for an HECM. You are also told to say that you want a lump-sum payment. But you never see the money because the con man has arranged to disappear with it at closing. If you didn't know that you were being conned, you're left with a big debt on a property that is worth a lot less. If you did know, or if someone suspects you knew, you're left with the debt and the real possibility of prosecution for fraud. Anyone considering a reverse mortgage needs to take extensive advice from a trusted lawyer. Accordingly, never deal with strangers bearing reverse mortgage, re-mortgage, or foreclosure rescue offers. Don't respond to unsolicited emails offering to save your home. Hang up on cold callers who phone you with a reverse mortgage or rescue scheme. And never participate in any compli-cated deal that you don't totally under-stand.

- **Low-Interest, No-Fee Credit Card.** The caller says he's from your bank, Visa, MasterCard, or any legitimate financial credit organization, and he's offering you a senior's-only credit card. He lists some basic qualifications — you have to be over a certain age, have lived at your current address more than six months, whatever — to make you feel that you've gotten past a real hurdle. He then explains how, having qualified, you are automatically preap-proved for a high credit limit. Also, the card carries no fees at all and has a special low interest rate designed for seniors. It means, he says, you can get rid of credit cards that have annual fees, transfer high-interest balances to this one, and save a lot of money. When you say, "Sign me up," he then explains that, unfortunately, there is a one-off charge of $200 for the application. If you say you're unhappy with that, some of these con men have been known to throw in the line that the $200 will be rebated if you transfer a balance onto the card or use it exclusively for six months. Naturally, it's nonsense. They say they have to debit the amount electronically from your bank account. If you balk, they will permit you to pay the fee with a different credit card. In any case, the new card will never show up because there is no new card. Instead, you may find that you are suddenly receiving all sorts of brochures and leaflets for cell phones, prescription drug programs, magazines, home redecoration loans, car loans, and free vacations that require you to pay an up-front fee. The con man has stolen your money and, as a thank-you, sold your name and address in a list of victims to other con men.

- **Funeral and Cemetery.** This is nothing more than a used car hustle by con men looking for a quick sign-here sale. They mine clients through affinity associations. Counting on seniors not to read the small print, they offer comfort, peace of mind, and what appears to be very cheap all-in-one package — casket, flowers, hearse, service, burial plot. Except that the small print is loaded with extra charges that turn out to be hugely expensive for the senior's heirs after the fact. And by then, it's too late for the senior to say, I didn't know. Legitimate funeral homes will always provide detailed price lists in writing and plenty of time to discuss the terms with family members. They will not pressure people into purchases, signing contracts, or paying excessive up-front fees.

- **ATM Helpful Stranger.** Those machines are not always easy to deal with, and it seems nice when someone kindly says, "Here, let me help you." Don't let him. These helpful strangers are simply trying to get inside your account. Also, it is essential to cover your hand when you enter your PIN as thieves have been known to place mini-cameras on ATMs to steal PINs. The best way to protect yourself is not to use outside machines, and if possible, never use private ATMs, like you find in supermarkets, corner stores, drug-stores, and many malls. It may not always be convenient, but it's always much safer to use the cash machine inside your own bank.

MEDICARE FRAUD

Among the many ways that fraudsters tap Medicare is by offering equipment — wheel-chairs, walkers, prosthetics, blood sugar monitors, breathers, and so on — free to seniors in exchange for their Medicare account number. The manufacturers then charge Medicare for the product, which might not have been needed or, for that matter, prescribed by your doctor. In certain instances, the equipment might not even be delivered to you.

Similarly, unscrupulous care providers — which can include doctors and hospitals — have been known to bill insurance for services they have not performed. And then there are rolling lab scams, which are fake tests given to seniors at health clubs, shop-ping malls, and sometimes even in nursing homes. These tests then get billed to Medi-care or an insurance company.

The only way you can prevent these things from happening is by closely monitoring the services and equipment you receive, never giving your insurance or Medicare number out to people you don't know, never signing blank forms, and never leaving boxes or spaces on forms unchecked or blank.

It is also important, before you purchase any Medicare prescription drug plan — no matter what the salesman tells you — that you understand these plans are voluntary and designed to supplement your Medicare benefits. Do not believe any sales pitch that says, if you don't join, you will lose your Medicare benefits. Furthermore, all prescription drug plans must meet specific federal standards as set down by the Department of Health and Human Services. Check first with Medicare at 800-633-4227 (TTY: 877-486-2048) or online (www.medicare .gov).

The law prohibits anyone marketing a drug plan to cold-call at your front door or send unsolicited emails. They are allowed to phone you to promote their plans, but they are not allowed to sign up a new client during the phone call. The government does not advertise or promote prescription drug plans, so any materials that appear to be from the government are not. All plans come with no strings attached. If a company offers you a cash rebate to enroll, that's illegal. It is also illegal if they offer a prize or gift for enrolling. Identity thieves often pose as salespeople and clerks from government offices. If someone contacts you claiming to be from Health and Human Services, or the Social Security Administration, or any other agency that you might deal with, and asks you to disclose bank account and credit card numbers, do not give them out. Government agencies will never ask for that information over the phone.

TEN TIPS TO HELP PROTECT SENIORS FROM FRAUD

1. If you didn't enter the contest, you didn't win it. No matter what anybody says about how the prize giver got your name, there is no such thing as a company you never dealt with, or person you never met, being so generous that all they want to do is give you something for nothing.

2. Your bank account is yours. If you let someone — especially a stranger — get close to it, they will steal from you. There is no reason for anyone to deposit money into your account, unless it's going to be your money. Anyone who wants to put money into your account, and then ask you to take it out on their behalf, is a crook.

3. Friends who call you on the phone are friends. Strangers who call you on the phone are strangers. You wouldn't give a perfect stranger who knocked on the door your credit card information; the stranger on the phone — or the stranger emailing on the Internet — is no different.

4. If a stranger on the phone asks to speak to the man of the house and there isn't one, the woman of the house should say, whatever it is, "*We're* not interested," and hang up. A woman should never admit she lives alone.

5. Never sign anything that you haven't read thoroughly and, where need be, shown to a lawyer or a close relative. No legitimate deal has to be signed for right away, regardless of how friendly the salesman seems to be.

6. If you're contracting with someone to do some work, check first with the local Better Business Bureau to make certain that the business is trustworthy. If they are, they will offer you a contract, which you should then have a lawyer read. If they are not, they'll try to talk their way around the contract and then ask for a fee up front. Legitimate companies don't do that.

7. There is no such thing as a legitimate investment that pays ten, twenty, or thirty times the current bank interest rate. The person offering you a guaranteed 2%, 3%, 4%, or 5% *a month* is a thief.

8. Never borrow money for any reason without letting a lawyer look at the terms of the deal.

9. Shred everything that has your name, address, Social Security number, or any financial information on it. Before throwing anything away — such as bills, notices, statements, and personal mail — shred it. Shredders are cheap, and identity theft, which can happen if a thief can find out who you are by going

through your garbage, can be financially lethal.

10. Don't discuss your life with strangers on the phone, even if they know your name. Just hang up. Use Caller ID to see who's calling. Or screen calls with an answering machine. If you get a lot of unsolicited calls, sign up for the National Do Not Call Registry. It's free (888-382-1222; www.donotcall.gov). Being on the registry won't solve everything, but it will help.

CHAPTER TWELVE: BUSINESS FRAUD

He was only a small player in the financial services industry, but the man who owned the firm was totally obsessed with keeping his assets secure, his employees honest, and his corporate reputation intact. He personally designed the various security systems to compartmentalize everything. If you worked on the second floor and had no business on the third floor, your pass wouldn't let you through the door up there. If your job didn't require access to certain computer files, your log-in code wouldn't allow you to get near those files. Everyone he hired was subjected to a strict vetting process, which included specialist testing designed to reveal a job candidate's deepest dishonest tendencies. He even went so far as to require handwriting analysis. He put strict spending limits in force, which meant if you were not authorized to move money, you couldn't. And if you were authorized — say, to pay bills or buy supplies — and it was more than your low-ceiling amount, he needed to know about it. If you went even close to corporate or client funds, authorized or not, red flags popped up on the computers of executives charged with oversight, especially his. With all those systems in place, he was certain that there was no way anyone could defraud him.

Except every night a cleaning crew came into the offices, and they had free access to the entire building, which meant that it was easy to steal company letterhead or place a key logger on selected computers or find someone's checkbook in an unlocked desk or copy billing and credit statements so they could order goods from regular suppliers or divert payments from regular customers.

When the fraudsters hit, it happened all at once.

And the man who owned the company couldn't understand how, despite his obsession with caution, he'd come so perilously close to losing it.

While all businesses are vulnerable to frauds of different sorts, small business can be particularly susceptible because many do not have the kind of controls — for payments, and so on — that larger companies have in place. Still, frauds involving businesses can be broken down into three broad categories: corruption or misuse of influence, which includes crimes like insider trading; falsification, which is misstatement of information, along the lines of the Enron fraud; and theft of assets, which is the Bernie Madoff fraud.

Overwhelmingly, fraud against companies usually pertains to theft of assets. And that can be broken down into two distinct categories: outside and inside.

FRAUDS FROM THE OUTSIDE
The most sinister fraud from the outside has to be online attacks.

A confidential letter from law enforcement to the banking industry a few years ago warned that cybergangs were actively stealing millions of dollars from businesses all over the world. In some cases, these were full-frontal attacks on computer systems. In others, they were managed with malware that was somehow planted inside a corporate computer system. No business was immune. And because most of these cybercrooks were operating out of eastern Europe, the chances of prosecutions and asset recovery were very low.

The problem has not gotten better over

the years. One reason might be because most businesses that get hit don't want to talk about it. The last thing they want is for their clients to suspect that a security breach might somehow jeopardize their own money.

All businesses need to do whatever they can to reinforce their computer defenses. But, by not sharing the problem openly, they are certainly not helping other businesses protect themselves or putting the perpetrators in jail.

Common frauds from the outside include variations on standard advance fee and identity theft scams, plus an array of false documentation fraud of which bogus invoices are a prime example.

Businesses generally have controls in place to deal with invoices from suppliers, contractors, and clients. But occasionally an invoice comes in that appears to be correct and isn't. If that invoice then slips by those controls, it might just wind up getting paid.

One popular bogus invoice scam is the fake ad renewal from Yellow Pages. It arrives in the mail, properly directed to the right office, and has the right Fingers Walking logo. Except that doesn't mean it has anything to do with your local Yellow Pages. There are business directories that call themselves Yellow Pages and use that logo, and some of them even get distributed somewhere. The bill even has a copy of last year's ad in the genuine Yellow Pages.

Along the same vein, scammers send out invoices for car, cleaning, and temp help services or for office supplies, hoping that someone will not think twice and pay it. The con man's theory is, send out enough of these and a certain percentage will get through.

One small business scam is an invoice for annual maintenance of the front-door entry system. If someone questions it, a few days later the front-door entry system is disconnected. In most cases, apologies from the business are accompanied by a money order payment.

Phony invoices frequently list a phone number — be suspicious of the ones that don't — and when you call to ask about the invoice, you get a convoluted explanation. Next comes the threat that if the invoice isn't paid on time there will be late payment interest and eventually, if it still isn't paid, it will be sent to a collection agency.

Because even a bogus unpaid invoice can cause confusion with your credit rating, that's when you need to call in the cops.

Paper and toner fraud is similar. Someone

claiming to be the regular office supplies company calls with some story about an overshipment coming in and no room to store it. He says he needs to get rid of it today, so if you want to buy some paper or toner very cheap — sometimes even below cost — this is the deal of a lifetime. The price is really low, he'll take a credit card, so you buy. Except he isn't your regular supplier and, chances are, there's no paper or toner on its way.

There are also several frauds that revolve around small business fax and phones. They include:

- **Fax Fraud.** A letter comes in by fax asking for information and prices about your business. Responding to it requires a lengthy return fax because there isn't any return address or other way to get the information to these people. And perhaps if it was a foreign number you might be less willing to respond, because that many pages going long-distance international can be expensive. But this appears to be a North American number. The problem is, not all North American numbers are created equal. Area codes in the Caribbean are all long-distance international from the United States. But some hide premium rate numbers, which can have extra charges because they are shared with the party being called. Suspicious area codes include, but are not limited to, 284 (British Virgin Islands), 649 (Turks and Caicos), 809 (Dominican Republic), and 876 (Jamaica). The fraudster is using what's known as a premium rate number, for which he receives a percentage on every call.

- **Pager Fraud.** A number comes up on your pager that you don't recognize, possibly with the word *emergency.* You return the call, get a recorded message, and hang up. But not before you are charged for a call to somewhere in the Caribbean, or elsewhere, at an exorbitant rate. Again, the fraudster is in on the take.
- **Slamming.** The business phone bill is suddenly double or triple what it usually is. When you study it, you don't recognize the name of the company providing the service. Unbeknownst to you, your long-distance service with the original carrier has been moved to another provider. In this case, it's the fraudster who has set himself up as a

service provider. He's actually gone into that business. But, being a crooked business, he has used your name and phone number to notify your original carrier that you wanted to switch. The original carrier had no idea it wasn't you asking to switch. So now you contact the new guy and say, what the hell is going on? He gives you the runaround before saying, but you authorized it. You say, not in this lifetime, pal. But then he produces a tape recording with someone in the business being asked questions like, are you happy with your long-distance service and would you be interested in taking advantage of our new plan? He claims that whoever answered yes committed you to the switch. Of course, that's not true. But it may cost you some money to get out of it. Your original carrier may charge you a fee for changing again, and the new guy may insist that you pay his bill. The way to prevent "slamming" from happening is to have the original carrier freeze your phone so that no one can switch it without your written permission.

When the theft of assets is orchestrated from the inside, fraud becomes a malignancy that can put otherwise viable businesses out of business and ruin countless lives.

Employees who steal have become a huge problem in America. One estimate suggests that fraud costs every business in the country $9 per employee per day. Another has it that the average business can expect to lose up to 6% of its annual revenue to fraud. Then, of course, there are those front-page headline frauds, along the lines of Enron, that bring a company to its knees and result in catastrophic systemic losses as well.

It's the bookkeeper who diverts funds into a relative's bank account, the manager who submits false invoices to commit check fraud, the salesman who puts personal items on his corporate credit card, and the warehouseman who's appointed himself a silent partner and ships goods out the back door for his own use or resale.

And yet, as significant as the problem is, disturbingly, very few businesses tend to report insider fraud to the police or press for prosecution. It's true that insider fraud can be difficult to detect and even more difficult to prove. Many insider scams go on for months or years before someone gets suspicious. And then, discovery often happens only by accident. The fraudster gets careless and copies an email to someone when he shouldn't or admits to knowing something that he wouldn't otherwise know or accidentally bumps into someone in the wrong place at the wrong time, when he's supposed to be someplace else.

Whatever finally exposes him doesn't necessarily matter because too many businesses worry more about reputational risk than punishing criminals. They don't want the publicity. They don't want their clients knowing that there's been a breach. Prosecutions can be lengthy and expensive, and if something goes wrong, lawsuits can follow. So, they reckon, it's best to solve these things quickly and quietly by recouping what they can and simply firing the employee.

Unfortunately, without prosecution, employees who have stolen in one company can get themselves on the payroll of another.

Of course, once someone is caught, that's when everyone who knows the case sees all the usual footprints in the sand:

- The perp had a lifestyle that didn't

match his income.

- He bypassed low bidders on obscure technical grounds and consistently awarded contracts to the same suppliers.
- He didn't take days off or vacations, like everybody else, as if he had to be in the office all the time to protect something.
- Records occasionally went missing, or seemed incomplete, and when anyone asked him if he knew anything, he got very defensive.
- He was frequently secretive about outside meetings and obviously jealous whenever anybody got close to his contacts.
- He'd be in his office with the door closed, using his cell phone, as if he didn't trust the company phone on his desk.

That list could go on and on. But there are other ways to look at these incidents.

Conventional wisdom has it that fraud thrives in businesses where there is no respect for controls. Or, perhaps it's more accurate to say that fraud thrives in businesses because there is always someone who figures out how to beat the system, at least for a little while.

If that's true, then the way to beat business fraud is to spot that person before he or she has the opportunity to beat the system.

In 1953, the late criminologist Donald Cressey surveyed some three hundred fraud perpetrators in prison, and concluded that when criminals commit a crime, they share three traits: motive, opportunity, and the ability to rationalize the misdeed.

Putting these three common traits in the context of business fraud, Cressey theorized that there might be one or two characteristics that could be used to identify an employee who might be more prone than another to commit insider fraud. And he came up with his concept of "unsharable problems."

Fraud by an employee is a crime of choice, but Cressey believed that very few people set out on the path of their working life with that in mind. That if they eventually commit fraud, it's because they're hiding a problem that they can't share with anyone else.

It may be an addiction — alcohol, drugs, gambling — or illicit affairs or some sort of consuming obsession. It may be financial — huge debts, not being able to live up to family expectations of income, living beyond one's means — or irresolvable marital problems. It may have to do with children or parents. It may be health related. Or it may be a combination of all these problems.

In fact, the nature of the problem matters less than the fact that the person has no one to share it with. There's no one to talk to at home, or he's too ashamed to tell anyone. He has no religious affiliations where he could get guidance and solace, or he feels that even if he trusted others enough to tell them, they wouldn't understand. When he comes to work every morning, his superiors say to his face, we don't care about your personal life, all we want out of you is a solid day's work.

His lack of loyalty to the business — and to the other employees — is easily rationalized by everyone's apparent lack of interest in his problem. Helping himself to some of the money in the till is easy, because he knows where it is, how to get his hands on it, and how to cover it up. And anyway, he now tells himself, I'll only take a little, kind of like a loan, and that will help relieve some of the problem. No one will know, and someday I'll put the money back and that will be the end of that, so it's not really stealing.

All these years after Donald Cressey first defined the term, it seems that if a business can find that employee with the unsharable problems and then do something like open the door to sharing, it might be making a significant step toward cutting down on insider fraud.

PART TWO

CHAPTER THIRTEEN: THE SCAMS

WHAT THEY ARE AND HOW TO STOP THEM

You protect yourself from fraud by looking at lots of frauds, by dissecting them, and by learning to spot the lie. It's not a difficult thing because when you look at enough of them, patterns emerge. Sure, there are tens of thousands — if not hundreds of thousands — of scams out there being used by con men in search of victims. And new ones are coming along every day. But you don't need to dissect all that many to see the patterns. Because once you understand the patterns, you can spot the lie.

AGENT FOR HIRE

THE SETUP: A foreign corporation is looking to do business in the United States and is offering you the opportunity to become its agent on the ground or to form a joint venture with a local partner.

THE LIE: They're not offering you anything; they're just trying to get you to pay them a fee.

THE SCAM: Here's an actual email, with all the original punctuation, spelling, and language use intact. Note the use of a legitimate company that has nothing to do with this fraud.

I am Engr. Robert Edmond the Purchasing Director of Tokyo Plastic Inc London. We wish to be in your country for a procurement and investment mission.

INTRODUCTION: Our company Tokyo Plastic Inc. has been a leader in production of all kinds of Plastic gems dolls and a leading supplier in solid mineral product in Europe, Its expertise and experience has provided mineral products to the major markets in America. Through her vast knowledge in solid mineral products of high quality we have provided the major markets with the products that are used as geological materials or High-powered optical lens.

PROPOSAL: We wish to come to your country for investment and procurement Mission. It has been our obligation to establish in Singapore especially in your country but due to political situation in Asia we left our priority in suspense but since the situation is better and confidence given to us based on your recommendation we wish to be in your country to meet with you and discuss issues in details.

2. DESCRIPTION: White in colour,

(a) Size: Irregular shape, like one cube of sugar

(b) Price per unit: $5100 US Dollars

(c) Quantity required: +60 162537795

NOTE: immediately we confirm the availability of this product and price Sold we will proceed down to meet with you for the purchase. You will assist to purchase this product, 10% of our total purchase will be paid to you as your commission for the assistance rendered.

You will sign a confidential non-circumvention, non-disclosure and agency representation Agreement. This agreement will run concurrently for 3yrs. You will become our only contact in Asia for purchase of this product.

Thanks for your anticipated assistance.

Best regards, Engr. Robert
Edmond(Purchasing Director)
TOKYO PLASTIC INC.LONDON

WEBSITE:WWW.TOKYOPLASTIC.COM
TEL: +447031841584 (Direct line)

WHAT'S REALLY HAPPENING: He's hoping you will fall for a really bad advance fee fraud.

HOW TO PROTECT YOURSELF: Read the letter carefully. None of it makes any sense. He seems to be looking for someone in Singapore, except he's sending this scam email all over the world. Apparently he wants you to buy a white thing of irregular shape, like a sugar cube, except that sugar cubes have very regular shapes. And whatever it is costs $5,100. It looks like he has more than 670 of them for sale, but then there's another number after 60, and who knows what that is. Although if it's a phone number, the country code is Malaysia. He says he's in Tokyo, has a London address and an Anglo name, but clearly doesn't speak native English. He also has a UK phone number — that's the +44 part — but he's using a 0703 number, which ties into a British service that diverts calls to anywhere in the world. It means he is not in the UK. He's an Engr, which supposedly means engineer, except that in English we don't use professional titles that way. But

236

they do use titles that way in Nigeria. Everything about this has scam written all over it.

VARIATIONS: All advance fee frauds wrapped around job applications and business partnerships look like this.

KEY WORDS: we wish to come to your country, investment and procurement, assist to purchase this product, your commission, confidential, non-circumvention, non-disclosure, agency representation agreement, our only contact.

COMMENT: Becoming his partner would be tantamount to tossing $5,100 out the window.

AREA CODE 809

THE SETUP: You receive a phone call, fax, pager message, or an email that asks you to get in touch. The message says you've won a prize, there is a problem with an account of yours, or a relative is ill or in some sort of trouble. Sometimes there is no message, just a callback number, left several times and at various hours, suggesting someone is anxious to reach you. The number you need to call begins with area code 809. You assume it's somewhere in the United States or Canada and make the call.

THE LIE: There is no prize, no account in trouble, no relative who's ill.

THE SCAM: You've been tricked into calling an overpriced international number, which happens to be in the Dominican Republic.

WHAT'S REALLY HAPPENING: The price per minute for the call is excruciatingly high, and the person on the other ends earns a percentage of your cost of the call.

HOW TO PROTECT YOURSELF: Unless you want to speak to someone in the Dominican Republic, don't return calls from area code 809.

VARIATIONS: Some of the porn lines that begin with area code 900 are rerouted through remote islands specifically to run up the cost per minute of the call. Same goes for areas codes 284 or 876.

KEY WORDS: area code 284, area code 809, area code 876, lottery, prize, your account, relative, urgent, callback, return the call, call immediately.

COMMENT: Because no one in the United States or Canada has to dial 011, the access code for an international call, it's easy to mistake area code 809 for a national call. If you receive a call from an area code you don't recognize that is supposed to be returned, check first where the area code is and what the calls cost. Also, while some phone systems can automatically block 900 numbers, they don't automatically block 809 numbers.

AUCTION PARCEL FRAUD

THE SETUP: After winning something in an online auction, the seller reminds you that the conditions of sale require you to wire payment to him. He says he understands that you may worry about doing that because you want to be sure that you get the item, so he offers to send it to FedEx, UPS, DHL or even the U.S. Post Office. He says they will check the purchase documents, guarantee everything is in order, and store it securely until payment is made. That way, he says, you have a third-party guarantee that you will get what you've paid for.

THE LIE: The courier services and post

office don't do any of the things the con man promises they do.

THE SCAM: You're paying for something you will never get.

WHAT'S REALLY HAPPENING: The seller sends you a courier shipment number to prove that the item has been sent. You now go to Western Union and send a MoneyGram with the payment. With your funds transfer number, you call the courier to arrange delivery. And they don't have a clue what you're talking about.

HOW TO PROTECT YOURSELF: Always pay with a credit card because that offers you some buyer protection. If you need a third party to intervene, use a reputable escrow service.

VARIATIONS: Parcel fraud works for more than just online auctions. Scammers do it all the time for big-ticket items, like cars, too, using a shipper instead of a courier.

KEY WORDS: guarantee everything is in order, store it securely until payment, third-party guarantee, funds transfer number, courier shipment number, FedEx, UPS, DHL, U.S. Post Office, Western Union, MoneyGram.

COMMENT: If a seller is suggesting a third-party payment arrangement, check with the third party to make sure they know about it.

BLACK MONEY

THE SETUP: You've lost money to a 419 scam and hounded the yahoo-yahoo boys (see Chapter 9) until they finally agree to return your money. A meeting in a neutral country is arranged with some prince and his entourage to apologize for the huge and regrettable mix-up. The money accidentally taken from your account will be returned immediately, he says, along with the promised $15 million fee. And best of all, the money is right there. They show you a stack of black paper, cut to dollar-bill size. Unfortunately, the explanation comes, because of Nigeria's currency rules that prevent the export of cash, they've had to overprint the money with a special black ink. That got the money through Nigerian export controls, and here it is. All you have to do is take this special black ink remover and wash it off each bill. Staring at a pile of

$15 million plus, even if all those hundred-dollar bills are covered in black ink, can be pretty convincing. At this point, some henchman pulls a piece of paper out of the stack, pours some liquid on it and, voilà, real money. All right, you say, thank you. I'll take it. "Good," the prince says, patting you on the back, "I'm glad we've settled this." Except, of course, you will need some ink remover. Unfortunately, they couldn't bring enough with them. Airline security and all of that. However, they promise they can get enough for you to do the job. But it's expensive. Luckily, however, there is someone who will sell it to you right around the corner. It will cost about $20,000 to remove all this ink, and, of course, the Nigerians will be right there to help you. So you'll just hand over twenty grand for the ink remover, and stay with the cash, they'll be right back.

THE LIE: Nothing has been smuggled out of anywhere or into anywhere else. There are only a couple of $100 bills in the stack; the rest of it is worthless photocopy paper cut to size.

THE SCAM: To prove it's really money, you're invited to pull a note out of the pile — pick a card, any card — at which time the man in charge uses an exotic chemical to erase the black ink. He hands you back a perfectly good $100 bill. They're all perfectly good, he says, but you'll have to use a lot of the cleaner to get through the piles of cash. And he just happens to have a friend who has plenty.

WHAT'S REALLY HAPPENING: The prospect of wealth beyond your wildest dreams clouds your better judgment when confronted with huge stacks of black paper. The pick a card, any card trick is just that, a simple magician's sleight of hand. If you have doubts after the first one, he's prepared to do it a second time, and a third time until you decide, hey, I'm rich. But then, there's that little problem of the detergent. So you hand over the twenty grand — or ten grand, or five hundred bucks, whatever you negotiate — and stay in the room with the money until he returns with the chemical. Needless to say, you'll be waiting there a very long time.

HOW TO PROTECT YOURSELF: This is a classic example of a back-to-back scam, having been invented by Nigerian 419ers as a way of bilking victims a second time. Keep away.

VARIATIONS: There is a copycat scam called white money where the bills are supposed to have been printed over in white ink.

KEY WORDS: black currency, black money, white money, ink, clean the bills, detergent, cleaner, special chemical, special liquid, smuggled.

COMMENT: If you've been bilked once by fraudsters, don't expect them to hand you back your money, no matter how sincere they appear to be. Given the opportunity, they will target you again, and again, and again. This kind of lightning can strike more than just once.

CHECK FRAUD

THE SETUP: You think you want to buy this "thing," but you're not 100% sure. Your dilemma is that this is a one-of-a-kind "thing." The fellow selling it is quick to point out that if you don't take it now, someone will definitely come along in the next few days to buy it out from under you. Except you feel uncomfortable being rushed into it. So he says to you, "I'll give you a few days to make up your mind. But as a show of good faith, you've got to give me a postdated check for the full amount." You date the check seven days from now, but you have to come back in three days to say yes or no, or he'll cash the check and you own it. (Or he says he'll take a check as a small deposit. If you come back in seven days and buy it, he'll deduct the deposit from the amount. If not, he gets to keep the deposit.) It sounds fair, so you write him a check.

THE LIE: This has nothing to do with selling you the "thing," it's about having one of your checks to play with.

THE SCAM: Given enough time, there are lots of way he can use your check to walk away with your money, and even your identity.

WHAT'S REALLY HAPPENING: Once he's got your check, he can wash out the amount that you've written, make it more substantial, and cash it, effectively stealing the new amount from you. Or he can forge a series of checks that are exactly the same as yours — thanks to home computers and digital printing, everything can be counterfeited — and hand those out, reaping as much as he can before your bank cottons on. Or he can do whatever he wants with your signature, like change your banking and credit card addresses and have a field day with your identity.

HOW TO PROTECT YOURSELF: Keep your checks to yourself. If you can, pay online or with a credit card or a cash card that will debit your account for the amount. If you pay online with electronic checks, be very careful because whoever you're paying now knows where your money is and the number of your account. Never allow your address or phone number to be printed on a check. Nor should you print your full name. Only use your first initial so that a forger has to guess. If you are going to pay with a check, use thick blue or black ink, and then make certain that you write large enough to fill the payee, amount, date, and signature lines. Don't leave enough space anywhere for someone to add something. If the person taking your check asks for your Social Security number, don't give it to him. Let him take your driver's license or other state ID number. And always keep your receipts. If a merchant offers to preprint your check by putting it through the register, do not sign it first. If you've made a mistake writing a check, write *VOID* across the front of it, rip it up, and take it with you to shred at home. If someone is paying you by check, suggest that a bank debit card is just as good. That guarantees your money right away, not when — and if — the check clears. Otherwise, try to hold the purchase until the check clears, which is not the same as the bank crediting you with the money before it actually arrives. And always insist on two forms of ID. Note the names, addresses, and numbers listed on both IDs on the back of the check.

VARIATIONS: Your signature can be forged on a check that has been printed by someone else to look exactly like your checks; a check you make out to someone can easily have the amount altered; a check that you've been given and already endorsed can have the endorsement changed and be used to pay someone else.

KEY WORDS: A check as a deposit; sign the check and we'll print it in the register; leave the payee blank and I'll fill it in later.

COMMENT: Only order checks from reputable printers, and if you lose a check, report it immediately to your bank. You might have to close the account and open a new one, but that's infinitely less hassle than having someone use your lost check to empty your account. Finally, if you pay certain bills with a check — credit card, utilities, cable TV, whatever — don't write your entire account number on the check. Use only the last four digits. No sense handing thieves more access to your life than they can get on their own.

CREDIT CARD EXPIRED

THE SETUP: The email from Visa (MasterCard, Diners Club, or American Express) reads like this:

> Your account has expired. You must renew it immediately or your account will be closed. If you intend to use this service in the future, you must take action at once! To continue CLICK HERE, log in to your account, and follow the steps.

THE LIE: Your credit card hasn't expired, and the email isn't from Visa, MasterCard, Diners Club, or American Express.

THE SCAM: This is a phishing scam, intended to panic you into handing over your credit card account number and password.

WHAT'S REALLY HAPPENING: The *click here* link leads you to a fake website, designed to look exactly like the real thing. When you enter your card details, you are actually turning them over to the fraudsters, who will take cash advances up to your credit limit.

HOW TO PROTECT YOURSELF: Your card clearly indicates valid dates on it, and that's when it expires. Before it does, the credit card company will issue you with another one. They will never send you an email with a *click here* link.

VARIATIONS: Suspicious charges have been put on your card; your card has been reported stolen; your account has been suspended; we are doing routine maintenance and need you to confirm your password.

KEY WORDS: expired, suspicious charges, stolen, suspended, routine maintenance, confirm your password, click here.

COMMENT: Never click on a link that comes from an unsolicited email.

CREDIT CARD II (OR CARD NOT PRESENT)

THE SETUP: You receive a phone call from your credit card company's fraud department, saying that there has been a security breach or some sort of unusual pattern of activity, and they need to check it. Of course you're suspicious. After all, how do you know who's actually calling. Except the caller knows your name and your address. He gives you his name and an employee reference number, says that if you have any doubts you should call the 800 number on the back of your card. And then he asks you to verify your card number — by reading the actual number to you.

THE LIE: The person calling claims to be from your credit card company but is probably from a business where you have previously charged something to that card or she has somehow obtained illegal access to your credit card number.

THE SCAM: The person calling already knows your name, your address, your phone number, and the number of your credit card. Despite the fact that it is easy, once someone has your name, to find your address, phone number, and other personal information, you figure because he's got all that this must be on the level.

WHAT'S REALLY HAPPENING: You're being lulled into a false sense of security so that you will now provide the one piece of information that the con men behind this scam don't have — the three-digit security code on the back of your card. Once they have that, they can then use your card on-line or by phone transaction as if it were theirs, reassuring vendors that they have the card in their possession. The three-digit security code or personal identification number (PIN) on the back of the card is there precisely to prove possession of the card.

HOW TO PROTECT YOURSELF: Be very careful to whom you divulge those three digits. Every purchase online that asks for you the security code, and every purchase over the phone that asks you to prove you have your card in your possession, adds to the risk that someone may then use it for what is known as card not present fraud — a purchase of something by someone other than the card owner, where the card itself isn't swiped or shown. Understand that, although the credit card companies do investigate strange activity on cards, to do that they don't need the three-digit security code. Nor do they need any other information. They already have it. If you suspect something, phone your credit card fraud department immediately.

VARIATIONS: The caller may say he's from your utility or cable TV company; it doesn't matter because the intent is the same. He will tell you anything he has to in order to get you to reveal the information he wants.

KEY WORDS: security code, three-digit PIN, unusual pattern of activity, usual purchases.

COMMENT: Never reveal credit card information over the phone to a cold caller. And if you buy something online, be especially vigilant.

DEBT ELIMINATION
THE SETUP: You find a website that advertises a seemingly perfectly legal way to eliminate (or radically reduce) your mortgage loan, bank overdraft, and all of your credit card debts. You contact them, tell them your story, and they say, no problem,

don't worry, we can make it happen for you.

THE LIE: No, they can't. The only ways that guarantee to eliminate debt are to declare bankruptcy, to die, or to pay it off. And then, most of the time, bankruptcy pays off some of it, and death merely passes it along to someone else.

THE SCAM: Advance fee fraud.

WHAT'S REALLY HAPPENING: With their guarantees and enthusiastic encouragement, you agree to let them handle your case. They now require all the information about your debts plus a special power of attorney that authorizes them to enter into whatever transactions they deem necessary on your behalf. They insist that you pay their fee in cash — which you must do face-to-face or through a wire service — and that can be anything upward of $1,500. And here's the kicker: They also take title to your house with an airtight promise that it will eventually be reassigned to you once the debt is clear. The company then issues bonds and promissory notes based on your house and claims that those actions legally satisfy all of your debts. But now, you're told, you also owe them a percentage of the value of those satisfied debts, otherwise you won't get your house back. In the meantime, there is a real possibility that they have also used all the personal information you've given them to run up more debt in your name.

HOW TO PROTECT YOURSELF: Do not get involved with anyone who promises to *eliminate* your debts.

VARIATIONS: debt management fraud, foreclosure fraud, ID theft.

KEY WORDS: perfectly legal, eliminate your mortgage, eliminate your bank overdraft, eliminate your credit card debts, power of attorney, issues bonds and promissory notes, legally satisfies all of your debts.

COMMENT: There are legitimate firms that will help you, but for every legitimate one, there are a thousand cons. Sorting the wheat from the chaff is not easy. The best people to speak to about help with eliminating your debts are the people to whom you owe the money, and your lawyer.

DEBT MANAGEMENT

THE SETUP: We can lower your interest rates, cancel your late fees, keep bill collectors away, stop constant harassment from credit agencies, and end your fear of going bankrupt.

THE LIE: If you're not paying your bills, there's nothing they can or will do about it.

THE SCAM: Crooked debt management agencies make wild claims to enroll customers who are facing bill collectors, credit agencies, and the real threat of bankruptcy, by promising to solve their problems, as if they had a magic wand. Unfortunately, the only way to put off the problem when it's reached this point is by setting up a repayment program with your creditors that will satisfy them. That means regular payments. Crooked debt management agencies are interested only in making you think they can end your problems, and for that — and the promise of being on your side, not your creditors' — they will charge you an upfront fee.

WHAT'S REALLY HAPPENING: It's advance fee fraud. They will sign you up as a client, possibly write a few letters on your behalf, be told by your creditors that whatever it is they're suggesting falls way short of actually paying off your debts in a sensible manner, and nothing will change. Except now you're also out the fee they charged you. Some of these scam agencies have been known to advise clients to stop paying their bills, but then never negotiated anything on their clients' behalf. Some agencies promise free debt counseling, but do little more than direct clients to other companies that charge high fees but rarely deliver on their promises. Crooked agencies regularly lie about the services they provide and the prices they charge.

HOW TO PROTECT YOURSELF: Before you pay any money up front, discuss the proposed debt management program with your creditors. Speak to your bank, and check with your lawyer. Check out the company offering debt management services with the Better Business Bureau. You need to know that the people you're dealing with are honest and have genuine professional references. If they're con men, it isn't going to work, and it is certainly not worth paying for. Your best choice, if you need debt counseling, might be to use a nonprofit agency that has a track record of helping consumers consolidate debts and negotiate lower interest rates. They will charge a fee, but it's nominal. Always check references.

VARIATIONS: We can reduce your credit card balance to zero, and we can keep the bank from foreclosing on your home. Some agencies offer free debt counseling but include hidden charges for the service.

KEY WORDS: lower your interest rates, cancel your late fees, debt management, bill collectors, harassment, credit agencies, going bankrupt, interest payments, consolidating debt, foreclosure, paying off your debts, debt counseling.

COMMENT: The last thing someone with severe debt problems needs is a con man stealing what little cash they may have left. Do not pay for services that have not yet been delivered. Deal only with legitimate firms. Your lawyer, your bank, and the Better Business Bureau can steer you in the right direction.

ESCROW

THE SETUP: You've sold something on an online auction, but the buyer wants to make certain that what you've sold him lives up to the description you put up before the sale. So he insists that the two of you use an escrow service until he can inspect the item and deem it as advertised. It's for your protection, too. What's more, he says he knows a very good escrow service that he's used before.

THE LIE: He's the escrow service.

THE SCAM: Escrow services are used all the time for buyer and seller protection, but the web is filled with phony escrow service sites, put up there by con men working on-line auction scams.

WHAT'S REALLY HAPPENING: You agree to use his service. The service notifies you that the payment has been made, and so you ship the item to the buyer. And that's the last you hear of him. He's got the goods and the escrow service doesn't return your emails.

HOW TO PROTECT YOURSELF: If you're going to use an escrow service, make sure it's reputable. Don't automatically believe the Better Business Bureau, VeriSign Secure, TRUSTe, or Internet Crime Complaint Center logos that show up on the service's home page. Fake escrow services use fake logos. If an escrow company doesn't have a physical address and listed phone number, don't go there. If it does, phone the number and ask where they're licensed. If you get only voicemail or they won't say where they're licensed, scratch them off your list. If they say they are licensed, check with the licensing authority. The problem is that once a phony site gets shut down, the fraudsters behind it quickly get back into the game somewhere else on the Internet with another name. You need to do your homework to find out who to trust.

VARIATIONS: Escrow services pop up in all sorts of other online businesses, not just auctions. The scam is the same.

KEY WORDS: it's for your protection, very good escrow service, I've used them before.

COMMENT: eBay advises that Escrow .com (www.escrow.com) is the only service they endorse.

FedEx (UPS, DHL, U.S. Postal Service)

THE SETUP: A postcard arrives, looking exactly like the card that FedEx leaves in your box when a package is not delivered — or it's an email — purporting to come from FedEx, UPS, DHL, or even the U.S. Post Office, saying that something valuable is waiting at their depot for you, and if you want it delivered, all you have to do is pay the fee.

THE LIE: There is nothing valuable waiting for you, and the postcard or email isn't from FedEx, it's from a Nigerian scammer.

THE SCAM: An actual email (with original spelling, grammar, and punctuation) reads:

Dear Valued Customer — We have been waiting for you to contact us for your Package that is been registered with us for shipping to your residential location. We had thought that your sender gave you our contact details. It may interest you to know that a letter is also added to your package. However, we cannot quote its content to you via email for privacy reasons. We understand that the content of your pack-

260

age itself is a Bank Draft worth of $800,000.00 (Eight Hundred Thousand US Dollars).

As you know, FedEx does not ship money in CASH or in CHEQUES but BANK DRAFTS are shippable. The package is registered with us for mailing by your colleague as claimed, and your colleague explained that he is here in West Africa for a three (3) month Survey Project as he works with a construction firm in Nigeria West Africa. We are sending you this email because your package is been registered on a Special Order.

What you have to do, is to contact our Delivery Department for immediate dispatch of your package to your residential address. Note that as soon as our Delivery Team confirms your information, it will take three (3) working days (72Hrs) for your package to arrive its designated destination. For your information, the VAT & Shipping charges as well as Insurance fees have been paid by your colleague before your package was registered.

You will have to pay the sum of $170.00 to the FedEx Delivery Department being full payment for the Security Keeping Fee of the FedEx Company as stated in our privacy terms & condition page Also be informed that your colleague wished to pay for the Security Keeping charges, but we do not accept such payments considering the fact that all items & packages that is registered with us have a time limitation and we cannot accept payment without knowing when you will be picking up the package or even respond to us. So we cannot take the risk to have accepted such a payment incase of any possible demurrage. Kindly note that your colleague did not leave us with any further information.

We hope that you respond to us as soon as possible because if you fail to respond until the expiry date of the foremost package, we may refer the package to the Appropriate Commission for Welfare as the package do not have a return address.

Kindly complete the below information and return it back to us. This is mandatory to reconfirm your Postal address and telephone numbers.

LEGAL NAMES: TELEPHONE: POSTAL ADDRESS: CITY: STATE: COUNTRY: AMOUNT TO SEND $170.00 ONLY:

As soon as your details are received, our delivery team will give you the necessary payment procedure so that you can effect the payment for the Security Keeping Fees. As soon as they confirm your payment of $170.00, they shall immediately dispatch your package to your designated address. It usually takes 72 Hours being an express delivery service. Note that we were not instructed to email you, but due to the high priority of your package had to inform you as your sender did not leave us with his phone number because he stated that he just arrived Nigeria West Africa and he was not on phone yet.

We indeed personally sealed your Bank Draft and we found your email contact in the attached letter as the recipient of the foremost package. Ensure to contact the delivery department with the email address above and ensure to fill the above form as well to enable a successful reconfirmation. Do not let anyone deceive you, because it is only $170.00 that you will need to pay to FedEx company to enable our delivery department deliver the parcel to your address.

God Bless you and have a Blessed day.
Yours Faithfully,
Mrs. Felicia Paul. FedEx Online Team Management.

WHAT'S REALLY HAPPENING:
Someone is trying to tempt you into sending them $170.

HOW TO PROTECT YOURSELF:
Throw the letter/email away.

VARIATIONS: UPS, DHL, U.S. Post Office, Lottery Fraud, Sweepstakes Fraud.

KEY WORDS: FedEx, valued customer, registered with us for shipping, cannot quote its content, bank draft, contact our delivery department, you will have to pay the sum of, necessary payment procedure, as soon as they confirm your payment, Nigeria, West Africa, do not let anyone deceive you.

COMMENT: Even by Nigerian scam standards, the grammar in the email is appalling and the tale is much too confusing. If it doesn't sound legit, it's not legit.

GOLD DUST

THE SETUP: Your new best friend Sam, whom you've never heard of, sends you this email (errors per original):

Dear Sir. We have 300 Kilograms in stock available for immediate sale. Our gold is 92% purity and 22 carats of best Ghana quality gold dust. The gold is for sale on FOB. Should you be interested, please contact us at: (samokoh55@yahoo.cn) for full corporate offers. Yours truly, Mr Sam Okoh

THE LIE: Sam doesn't have any gold dust, because if he did, there is an established market for it; he doesn't need to flog it to strangers.

THE SCAM: Advance fee fraud.

WHAT'S REALLY HAPPENING: Sam explains this part of it better than anyone else. When you write to him to say you're interested, this is how he answers (again, errors per original):

Dear Sir, Thank you very much for your valued inquiry. Yes, we have 300kgs of Gold Dust for sale. Our price is $12,500 per a kilo base 22 carat and 92% as purity. Procedures: (1) You will come to Ghana to inspect our product first. Then if you are satisfied with our product, that is, after test, we discuss terms of supply and payment in the MOU. (2) We can give you a trial shipment between 5-10kgs or less but you will pay us enabling money as export fees. You will deduct the repaid export fees from our final balance after receive, tested, and refined. Note, we will pay here to have legal backing should you receive this trial shipment and fail to pay our balance. If this second option is good for you, send to me a scan copy of your passport or Driver's license, the address receives this trial shipment, a confirmation of address from any of the Utility services in your country like phone bill etc. I expect your quick response. Regards, Okoh.

HOW TO PROTECT YOURSELF: Unequivocally, never send your passport, driver's license, utility bill, and $37,500 to anyone named Sam in Ghana. Or anyone else in Ghana. Or anyone else anywhere.

VARIATIONS: If it's not gold dust, it's petroleum. If it's not Ghana, it's Sierra Leone. If it's not Sam, it's Barrister Regan.

KEY WORDS: inspect our product, satisfied with our product, trial shipment, pay us enabling money, export fees, a scan copy of your passport or driver's license, confirmation of address from any of the utility services in your country.

COMMENT: As hard as it is to believe, people do fall for this crap. And even if the potential victim is careful enough not to send money right away, once he's sent a copy of his passport, driver's license, and utility bill, he's in for trouble anyway.

HITMAN FOR HIRE

THE SETUP: A voicemail, note, or email arrives with this very upsetting message: "I have been paid to kill you."

THE LIE: Not likely. Mafia hitmen don't tend to warn their victims first.

THE SCAM: The message goes on, and the scam quickly becomes evident. The assassin confesses: "I took the contract to kill you but feel bad about it. After all, I don't know you. But the people who want you dead have already paid me. If you want to pay me more, I'll back off. Otherwise, you're dead."

WHAT'S REALLY HAPPENING: This is called *extortion.* Someone is threatening you for money. To convince you that he's for real, he may send you surveillance photos of you taken at a distance, or information about your personal life. He may even offer to tell the police who hired him to kill you. But before he does that, and instead of pulling the trigger, you've got to pay him off.

HOW TO PROTECT YOURSELF: Immediately call the cops.

VARIATIONS: The hit might not be on you. It could be your spouse, parents, children, grandchildren, even your pet.

KEY WORDS: kill you, want you dead, pay me.

COMMENT: Most people go through their entire life without ever once being targeted for murder. And if something like this happens, it's easy to assume it's a scam or some sort of bad joke. No good. Let the police decide exactly what this is and, if necessary, take action.

HOME FORECLOSURE

THE SETUP: You've fallen behind on your mortgage payments and are approached by someone offering a foreclosure rescue scheme. These people will pay off your mortgage and allow you to stay in your home by renting it back to you. They will also give you an option to purchase your home from them at a later date.

THE LIE: They will not pay off your mortgage.

THE SCAM: The rescue requires you to deed your home to someone, usually a third party who is introduced to you as an investor but is party to the scam. Your rental payments will go to him — and that's the last you'll see of your money.

WHAT'S REALLY HAPPENING: The so-called investor, who has found your name in public foreclosure listings, will not make your mortgage payments for you. Instead, he sells the house on to someone else, stripping the equity out of it. When the bank comes looking for its mortgage payments, he's long gone and you're evicted.

HOW TO PROTECT YOURSELF: Never sign documents without first consulting an attorney, and then never sign anything with blanks or obviously false statements. Never do business with anyone who promises to repair your credit rating, pay your costs, or buy your home quickly. These things always take a lot of time. They simply cannot be done in a few days. Never do business with any self-styled consultant who insists you pay up-front fees. Never make mortgage payments to anyone except your mortgage lender. Never transfer your property title without first speaking to your mortgage lender and then only in the presence of an attorney. While there are legitimate mortgage consultants, never enter into a negotiation with anyone before checking with the Better Business Bureau or your state attorney general's office.

VARIATIONS: If it's not your mortgage, this will work with any property of value, such as a car.

KEY WORDS: pay off your mortgage, deed your home, rescue package, repair your credit rating, pay your costs, buy your home.

COMMENT: Never entertain any unsolicited offers from strangers — by phone call, mail, or email — touting a rescue package.

HOME FORECLOSURE II: THE LAND PATENT

THE SETUP: "We can save your home for you with the unique and little-used device called a land patent."

THE LIE: Owning a land patent voids

mortgages and property taxes.

THE SCAM: Sold through seminars and classified ads, this foreclosure scheme is based on the falsehood that land patents, otherwise known as land grants, legally turn the ground under your home into a sovereign nation. As such, you are forever protected from the bank because this is no longer U.S. territory. The theory is that if the mortgage lender cannot own the land, any home built on it is useless, and they will therefore not foreclose.

WHAT'S REALLY HAPPENING: You are being sold pie in the sky. Even if you could somehow declare your land to be sovereign, which is very difficult to do, it postdates your mortgage contract and therefore will not be considered legal by the mortgage lender or the courts.

HOW TO PROTECT YOURSELF: Avoid anyone offering a magic pill to solve your foreclosure difficulties. And before acting on any offer, consult your attorney.

KEY WORDS: land patent, sovereign territory.

COMMENT: The more gimmicky the solution, the more suspect it should be.

Hot Stock Tips

THE SETUP: "Insider trading is against the law, and although we got this from the inside, you're getting this tip on a publicly available blog, so it is perfectly legal for you to buy ABCD Industries. It's currently trading at 6¢ a share, but the company is about to be taken over and when that happens, the stock could trade as high as $1. Since we've been touting it, shares have already increased 50%."

THE LIE: No one is taking over the company. The blogger touting the shares either owns them, is trying to sell shares that he controls, or is selling shares on which he'll get a commission.

THE SCAM: Websites, blogs, chat rooms, and emails are overflowing with hot stock tips for shares that are going nowhere. But you never know what conflicts of interest are driving these hucksters.

WHAT'S REALLY HAPPENING: The blogger is promoting ABCD Industries because he's probably stuck with shares that he wants to dump or he's going to get a substantial commission. He needs to goose up the price. The 50% gain he's reporting could be from 4¢ to 6¢ because a few people may be buying on the rumors the blogger is spreading.

HOW TO PROTECT YOURSELF: Never invest off the back of tips on the Internet.

VARIATIONS: Bloggers who tip shares, bonds, metals, commodities, horses, sporting events, anything and everything count as a "net tip." But the scam works just as well by word of mouth from an "inside" source, who just happens to be selling or buying, or has a close friend who is. You find this happening at clubs, benevolent associations, church groups, and so forth.

KEY WORDS: can't fail, take over, must go up, get in now, no time to waste.

COMMENT: Most Internet tips are based on wishful thinking and conflicts of interest, not real knowledge.

INHERITANCE

THE SETUP: Someone died and left a lot of money to his distant relative who needs your help collecting it.

THE LIE: There is no distant relative, and there is no inheritance.

THE SCAM: The person who stands to inherit all this money — and the figures always run into the millions — needs your help getting the money out of some difficult place in the world, and for your help he will pay you one-third. All he needs to do is be able to wire the money into your bank account.

WHAT'S REALLY HAPPENING: This is just another way the Nigerians work 419 fraud.

HOW TO PROTECT YOURSELF: Never give anyone your banking information and never let anyone use your bank account.

VARIATIONS: The advance fee fraud variation has it that the distant relative needs to hire lawyers and pay taxes in order to get the money. If you will send him one-third of his fees, perhaps several thousand dollars, he will give you one-third of his inheritance, which he promises is several million. Yet another variation, also advance fee fraud, is that he has stumbled onto the fortune left by someone famous, it is unclaimed by the famous person's family, and he wants you to become a partner in claiming it, of course for a fee.

KEY WORDS: inherit, pay you one-third, into your bank account, become a partner, unclaimed.

COMMENT: Why would someone you don't know send an email to someone he doesn't know — he doesn't even know your name — and offer you all this money?

IRS FORM W-9095

THE SETUP: A letter arrives from the IRS saying that during their review of last year's tax return, you failed to include Form W-9095, "Application for Certificate Status/Ownership for Withholding Tax." A copy is enclosed, which must be completed and faxed back within seven days.

THE LIE: There is no form W-9095.

275

THE SCAM: Fraudsters are looking to empty your bank account and/or run an ID fraud with your name.

WHAT'S REALLY HAPPENING: The W-9095 looks almost exactly like a legitimate Form W-9, "Request for Taxpayer Identification Number and Certification." Except that the W-9 only asks for your name, address, and Social Security number. The W-9095 wants your bank account number, marital status, date of birth, place of birth, parents' names, Social Security number, work details, and, if you have one, a photocopy of your passport.

HOW TO PROTECT YOURSELF: Do not respond. Instead, find the closest IRS office — get their number from a phone book or online, and definitely not from the letter accompanying the W-9095 — and tell them what's happened. They will then tell you which IRS criminal investigation division office to send the blank form, cover letter, and envelope. Otherwise, phone the IRS customer service hotline, 800-829-1040.

VARIATIONS: A similar letter comes from a bank, with the form enclosed, explaining that the bank is required by the IRS to notify all their clients. The bank warns that if the form isn't completed on time, they will be forced to withhold 31% of all earned interest. Other forms that have been used in this scam are the W-88BEN and W-8888. In fact, there is a legitimate version of the W-88BEN, which banks do send out, but the scammers' fake version asks for much more personal information.

KEY WORDS: IRS tax form W-9095, W-88BEN, W-8888, required by the IRS, taxpayer identification number.

COMMENT: The IRS will write to you by name, with your tax ID or Social Security number on the letter. They will never email you. And if they do phone you, it will almost always be in response to your having phoned them, and then they will never ask for personal information such as bank account numbers and passwords.

IRS REFUND
THE SETUP: The typical email reads:

After the last annual calculations of your fiscal activity we have determined that you are eligible to receive a tax refund of

$63.80. Please submit the tax refund request and allow us 6-9 days in order to process it. A refund can be delayed for a variety of reasons. For example submitting invalid records or applying after the deadline. To access the form for your tax refund, please <u>CLICK HERE</u>. Regards, Internal Revenue Service

THE LIE: There is no refund.

THE SCAM: *Click here* and you wind up on a phony IRS page where you are requested to fill out a form with all your personal details.

WHAT'S REALLY HAPPENING: It's identity theft.

HOW TO PROTECT YOURSELF: Never click on a link of any unsolicited email.

VARIATIONS: The amount of the refunds may vary, and the reason for the phony refund can vary, too: to help resolve unresolved tax problems, as the result of a tax avoidance investigation, or after having calculated the taxpayer's fiscal activity. One version offers an $80 fee to anyone willing to complete an IRS online customer satisfaction survey. Another is addressed to businesses who are considered to be tax-exempt organizations. Fake emails also come from the IRS Antifraud Commission, which doesn't exist.

KEY WORDS: tax refund, eligible to receive a tax refund, submit the tax refund request, click here, overpaid taxes, economic stimulus, exempt organizations, unresolved tax problems, fiscal activity, online customer satisfaction survey, tax avoidance investigation, IRS Antifraud Commission.

COMMENT: The IRS *never* contacts people by email.

JURY DUTY

THE SETUP: A letter or email arrives, with your name and address clearly spelled out, plus a case number. It's on official-looking stationery, or has some sort of official-looking logo in the email, and comes from the official-sounding jury duty selection office. There is a return address — often a post office box — plus a phone number that, when you call it, is picked up by an answering machine. The letter or email informs you that a warrant has been issued for your arrest. The charge against you is failure to appear after having been summoned by the courts for jury duty.

THE LIE: You weren't summoned, there is no arrest warrant, and jury duty and the courts don't operate this way.

THE SCAM: The correspondence is from an official-sounding body: State of New Jersey, State Court Sheriff, Colorado State Court Jury Summons Office, Office of the Clerk of the Courts of the State of California, Texas State Warrant Issuing Office, Central Summonsing Bureau for the State of New York, Courts of Justice, and so on. It explains that sometime ago (90 days, 120 days) a notice was sent to you requiring attendance for jury duty. When you did not appear, a second notice was issued. When you failed to respond to that, a third notice was sent giving you a fixed amount of time (say, 21 days) to explain to the courts why you have disregarded those previous notices. The correspondence you've just received goes on to explain how it was clearly spelled out at the time that, should you fail to respond to the third notice, an arrest warrant would be issued. And now it has been. The threat of jail is enough to scare most people, especially when you never received any of that previous correspondence. Of course, the reason you didn't get it is because it doesn't exist. You are relieved to see that the very next paragraph suggests that the correspondence might have been sent to you in error and that the jury notice — and subsequent arrest warrant — might actually be for somebody else. If that's the case, you are instructed to go to a website or phone a hotline (which takes recorded information) and prove your innocence. To do that, the website or phone prompts ask you to provide certain personal information: name, address, phone number, Social Security number, banking details, and the like.

WHAT'S REALLY HAPPENING: Someone is attempting to panic you into giving him whatever he needs to empty your bank account.

HOW TO PROTECT YOURSELF: No one is summoned for jury duty, anywhere in the United States, by email. Names are taken off the voter registration lists and sent by snail mail. If you receive such notification, it's easy enough to check with the clerk of the court, whose number is available in phone books, on the web, and through directory assistance. Do not call the number provided in the email or letter. Once you have verified that you have not been summoned, phone your local police, get the name of an officer who deals with fraud, and pass the notification on to him.

KEY WORDS: arrest, warrant, failure to appear, prove your identity, required details, bank details, Social Security number, credit card details.

COMMENT: Under no circumstances should you respond to the notice. And never, ever provide personal information to anyone over the phone or through emails, even if they claim to be a court official.

Loss Recovery

THE SETUP: You've lost money in an advance fee fraud, and complained about it enough that when someone contacts you out of the blue about it, you're not at all suspicious. He says he's lost money, too, from the same scam and has figured out a way to get his money back. He wants to know if you're interested in getting your money back, too.

THE LIE: He hasn't lost money. He's the scammer.

THE SCAM: He says he's putting together a small group of like-minded victims, has a lawyer on board, and may have to hire a private detective. But he insists he knows who the con man is, where he is, and where his assets are. He says the first thing he wants to do is seize the assets, then he will press for the police to arrest him. But to do this, he needs partners, which means they have to split the expenses.

WHAT'S REALLY HAPPENING: There is a belief among con men that if they can get you once, they can get you twice. And this time, they know the perfect way in — your anger with having been hit the first time.

HOW TO PROTECT YOURSELF: By all means use whatever legal means you've got to recoup your losses, if you can. But an unsolicited offer from someone you don't know looking for money? Probably not.

VARIATIONS: If it's not one victim, it's a victims' support group, or someone claiming to be an attorney/private detective working for the victims.

KEY WORDS: small group of like-minded victims, seize the assets, share the expenses.

COMMENT: In matters like this, your first loss is usually your cheapest.

LOTTERY

THE SETUP: An email arrives to congratulate you on winning the Euromillion Loteria Award.

THE LIE: There is no Euromillion Loteria, you didn't win, and there is no prize.

THE SCAM: The email reads (including original errors):

> We wish to congratulate you over your email success in our computer balloting sweepstake held on [date]. This is a millennium scientific computer game in which email addresses were used. It is a promotional program aimed at encouraging internet users; therefore you do not need to buy ticket to enter for it. Your email address attached to ticket star number (45407) with serial number 51622 drew the EUROMILLION lucky numbers 3-18-

40-40-76 which consequently won the draw in the Second category. You have been approve for the star prize of €667,248.26.

The use of double-talk like "millennium scientific computer game" is to convince you that you've won a lottery you've never heard of. What's more, the idea of needing to encourage people to use the Internet is bizarre, given the fact that worldwide, the Internet gets used by more people than does toothpaste. The email then goes on to warn:

You are advised to keep this winning confidential until you receive your lump prize in your account or optional check issuance to you. This is a protective measure to avoid double claiming by people you may tell as we have had cases like this before.

In other words, don't tell anyone who might smell a scam. Now comes the pitch for your personal information:

Please send your Full Name, Home and Office Tel & Fax Number, Mobile Tel Number and your winning ticket number, reference numbers and amount won information for processing of your winning fund to our registered claim agent.

The email itself is signed by the "lottery coordinator" and is followed by a reference number to make this all look real: "Ref. N°: ESM/WIN/008/05/10/MA Batch. N°: EULO/2907/444/908/06." For good measure, there's a reassuring PS:

This promotional program takes place every year. This year lottery was promoted and sponsored by THE MANAGEMENT OF THE STAATSLOTERIJ COMPANY B.V. AND SULTAN OF BRUNEI, we hope with part of your winning you will take part on our next year €2 million international lottery.

The use of names like the Sultan of Brunei is to give the scam some semblance of legitimacy. Other names that turn up are Bill Gates, Microsoft, Arnold Schwarzenegger, Queen Beatrix of the Netherlands, King Juan Carlos of Spain, Nelson Mandela, and Warren Buffett. Needless to say, none of these people are involved or have any idea their names are being used.

WHAT'S REALLY HAPPENING: The fraudsters are mining your personal information or playing off your greed to extract an advance fee. If you contact the agent, you will be instructed to supply your banking details because local legislation requires that they must wire your winnings from their bank to yours, or send them a certain sum of money, say $300, as a processing fee, shipping fee, handling fee, or to simply pay for the "Legalization and Endorsement charges." In the first scenario, they'll empty your bank account. In the second, they'll disappear with your $300.

HOW TO PROTECT YOURSELF: Delete the email or, if you really want to play the lottery, buy a ticket for a legitimate one.

VARIATIONS: There are thousands of phony lottery scams running through the Internet, including the Canadian National Lottery and one called Global Software Promotions. Whatever they're called, all of them use the same technique. They all explain why you never heard of the lottery you supposedly just won, and that to collect the prize, you have to notify them or their agent and supply information or money.

KEY WORDS: dear prize winner, congratulate you, congratulations, computer sweepstakes, aimed at encouraging, lottery, computer generated, your email address, confidential, to avoid double claiming, did not need to buy a ticket, did not need to enter, in order to collect, contact our agent, promotional program, promotional draw, selected through a computer ballot system, our security protocol, Canadian National Lottery, Global Software Promotions, final winning notification, lump-sum payout.

COMMENT: Be highly suspicious of any email that has been sent to "undisclosed recipients."

LOW-INTEREST GUARANTEED LOAN

THE SETUP: Ads in newspapers and all over the Internet offer low-interest guaranteed loans for personal or business use, irrespective of a borrower's credit history.

THE LIE: It's not a loan, it's an advance fee scam.

THE SCAM: They give you a number to call to ask for application forms, which demand a lot more personal information than any bank or finance company would request, including bank and credit card information, Social Security number, and copies of your driver's license and passport.

As soon as you send the forms back, you receive a call that you've been approved for the loan. That's when you're told that there are some minor fees to be paid, including insurance, processing, and three months' interest plus three months' principal repayment. That money has to be wired to the loan company before any money is sent to the borrower.

WHAT'S REALLY HAPPENING: The loan company is a fraudster playing off extremely desperate people. They steal the insurance and processing fees, plus the advance interest and principal repayments. Telltale signs include his lack of a four-walls-and-roof address, and haste. He will do whatever he can to rush you into taking out the loan. He will also double-talk his way around any information about the company, where it is located, and what professional association memberships they hold.

HOW TO PROTECT YOURSELF: If you need a loan, deal only with reputable lenders, never anyone whose only point of contact is a phone number or address in cyberspace.

VARIATIONS: The promise of a loan that will never happen is used not only for personal or business reasons, but also for school grants and to discount invoices and letters of credit.

KEY WORDS: low interest, guaranteed, personal or business use, insurance fee, processing fee, irrespective of a borrower's credit history.

COMMENT: No legitimate lender can guarantee a loan and ignore a borrower's credit rating. And it is illegal for any lender to ask for repayment of any portion of a loan before the loan is even granted.

MISSED PHONE CALL

THE SETUP: Your cell phone rings once. You go to answer it, but whoever's calling has suddenly hung up. There is, however, a "missed call" number. So on the off chance that it's important, you call back.

THE LIE: No one actually phoned you, and the offer you're about to get doesn't actually exist.

THE SCAM: You check the missed call number and dial back. A woman answers with something like, "Holiday line . . . Customer service." You ask what that is and why they phoned you. She explains that it might be about a holiday, asks you for your cell phone number, and pretends to look it up. "Oh," she says, "terribly sorry that we got cut off, but, yes, we were trying to reach you to explain that you've won a holiday for two, all expenses paid, to [pick a place]." The Seychelles? Bahamas? Greece? Thailand? You ask, "How come I won this?" And she gives you a lengthy explanation that might include anything from the credit card you use or your cell phone provider. Whatever, it sounds plausible enough that you start asking for details. She now tells you that she's only the help desk, and that for specific details, you'll have to speak to the prize desk. Either she passes you along to someone else — which takes some time and you wind up spending a few minutes listening to canned music — or you're told you have to dial another number. In both cases, a man now goes through a long spiel asking you for all sorts of information, before saying that there might be some confusion about the prize. You try to convince him that the Seychelles (Bahamas, Greece, Thailand) for two, all expenses paid, is what you've won, and the conversation continues.

Eventually, the man takes your mailing details and promises to be in touch. When the prize finally arrives, it's a discount coupon on a holiday that you have to buy. So now you call back and speak to someone else, and listen to more canned music, spending a lot of time trying to find out where your prize is.

WHAT'S REALLY HAPPENING: Your number has been dialed by a computer, which generates tons of calls a day. In some of these scams, computers can dial a million numbers in a weekend. When you phone the missed call number on the screen, you're actually calling a premium rate line. In some cases, those lines are not even in the United States. So, without knowing it, you might also be making an overseas call. For the right to hear about a prize you're never going to receive, you'll be paying $1 to $7.50 per minute. Through arrangements with some telephone service providers, a number of them in foreign countries, the con men will make a sizable percentage of whatever premium rate fees are charged. And these calls can last anywhere from a few minutes to more than an hour. How long they can keep you on the line depends entirely on how good they are, and how gullible you are.

HOW TO PROTECT YOURSELF: If you don't recognize the number of the missed call, don't call back. If it was really important, whoever phoned you wouldn't let it ring only once or will try you again.

VARIATIONS: If it's not a phone call, it's a text message. Again, these are computer generated and ask you to call a number immediately.

KEY WORDS: missed call, call this number, area code 809.

COMMENT: Never assume that a call that appears to come from a cell phone or even a landline is just that. Digital technology being what it is, premium rate numbers can now be disguised so you don't realize you're being charged until you get the bill.

MYSTERY SHOPPER

THE SETUP: Do you love to shop? Why not get paid for it? Retailers across the country are looking for people to assist their marketing research and help them evaluate the quality of service in their stores. Shop till you drop, report on how well you were treated, and the store will either pay you a fee or allow you to keep what you've bought. Interested? Pay us, and we'll show you how.

THE LIE: Legitimate marketing research firms and retailers don't require a fee to find out how to become a mystery shopper.

THE SCAM: Once you register, you will be charged an application fee, a fee for a directory of retailers supposedly hiring secret shoppers or a mystery shopper certificate, which pretends to be a license and is completely bogus.

WHAT'S REALLY HAPPENING: You're being set up for an advance fee fraud or an overpayment scam, or both.

HOW TO PROTECT YOURSELF: There is an organization called the Mystery Shopping Providers Association (MSPA), and if this is what you want to do, they'll tell you how (www.mysteryshop.org). They warn that the MSPA never seeks to recruit shoppers or asks for payment from them to conduct work. Anyone who does should be considered suspect.

VARIATIONS: You are hired by a major

retailer, such as Walmart, to secretly test their money wire service. You receive a check for $3,000, which you must deposit into your account. You are then told that you can take out of that $500 — which is two hours' work at $250 an hour — and must then wire the remaining $2,500 from Walmart to an address provided. Of course, this is just another overpayment scam. The check you've deposited into your account is bogus, and you now owe your bank the $2,500 you've just sent to the fraudsters. Or they send you a check that is supposedly to pay for goods that you buy. But here, too, the check is counterfeit.

KEY WORDS: love to shop, secret shopper, earn money while shopping.

COMMENT: Beware of deals that require you to pay up front to get a job. And never permit anyone to use your bank account.

MULTILEVEL MARKETING

THE SETUP: Make $500 a week mailing postcards.

THE LIE: You're not actually buying into his scheme, you're paying for the right to buy in, and no matter how you work it, the numbers don't add up to a profit for anybody, except the guy selling the scheme.

THE SCAM: The pitch claims that this is foolproof. All you have to do to make $500 a week is follow the instructions of the man who runs this multilevel marketing (MLM) scheme. It's a perfectly simple system, he says. The postcards you will mail invite people to make $500 a week sending out postcards. You pay him $30 for the chance to be in business with him, and in return, he promises you will make $20 for every new client he gets thanks to your postcards and a follow-up letter. So you decide to send five hundred postcards, which means you need to have them designed and printed. Put that cost at $50. Then you need five hundred addresses. If you could even buy a mailing list that small from a direct mail operator — these are people who sell lists of a hundred thousand or more — they'd charge you at least 8¢ to 10¢ per name. Let's say you got five hundred at the rock-bottom 8¢ price, that's $40. Now you've got to pay postage, which at 28¢ per, costs $140. You've now invested $260. The average cold call direct mail response is 1% to 2%. Taking the high side, let's say you get ten responses for your five hundred postcards. You now have to send those people a follow-up letter, explaining that they must send your partner $30 to learn how they can have the chance to make $500 a week sending out postcards and a follow-up letter to people who might want to make $500 a week sending out postcards. The MLM guy insists that selling the right to sell the right can bring in a 16% return. It's unlikely but possible. So your ten letters now bring back about one and a half, call it two, responses. For which you earn $20 each. But don't forget, you've also had to pay for the follow-up letters and the postage. But even if you don't factor those in, your $500 gain is actually a $220 loss.

WHAT'S REALLY HAPPENING: Multilevel marketing is not always a scam. But when you're selling the right to sell the right, and there is no product, it's no different than a chain letter.

HOW TO PROTECT YOURSELF: Don't waste your time with *any* get-rich-quick schemes.

VARIATIONS: Pyramid schemes and chain letters.

KEY WORDS: foolproof, selling the right to sell the right.

COMMENT: There is no way these schemes can work, except for the fellow at the top of the MLM food chain. Everybody else is always hustling to lose less, and paying him for the privilege.

OVERPAYMENT

THE SETUP: You've sold something for $700 through Craigslist or on eBay, but the buyer sends you a check for $1,000 in error.

THE LIE: The overpayment is not an accident, and the check is no good.

THE SCAM: After advertising on Craigslist, or in your local paper or on the Internet, you've finally sold a family heirloom — or a car, or a piece of furniture, whatever — for $700. The buyer sends you a check for $1,000. Sorry, he says, I sent you the wrong amount by accident. Or he sends you a third-party check, claiming it's money he's owed that he can't deposit in his own account without having to pay tax on it. He's even willing to let you take an extra few bucks for cashing it. Go ahead and deposit it, he says, and when the check clears, just send me the difference. It's no problem, he insists, I trust you. You're glad to get rid of whatever it is you've sold, and there's no apparent risk to you because you're going to wait until the check clears before sending him the goods and the overpayment. So you take the check and deposit it, and two or three days later you see that your bank has credited you with $1,000. The check cleared, so you hand over the goods and the $300 difference.

WHAT'S REALLY HAPPENING: You've just been bilked for the value of the goods you've sold, plus $300 that you've been told to wire back to the con man. Con men insist on wires because they don't trust your checks. And they should know. *Their* checks are either stolen or counterfeit. But you and your bank didn't know that when you deposited it. What your bank does is put it in the system and, after a few days, credits you with that amount. That doesn't mean, however, that the funds have cleared and are actually in your account. It simply means your bank has made a paper transaction and is advancing you the money in the belief that they are about to receive the money. The bank won't get its hands on the money for five to seven days. If the money is drawn on a foreign bank, they will have to wait even longer. So the bank has made a good-faith transaction to you, which means that as soon as the bank finds out the check is no good, they turn around and debit the money they've already put in your account. Of course, by that time, the fraudster is long gone.

HOW TO PROTECT YOURSELF: Never accept third-party checks, never accept overpayments — even if the person handing you the check, or any financial instrument, promises you a cut of the overpayment — and never hand over anything of value to the person who gave you the check until your bank assures you that the deposited funds have cleared and are also secure in your account. Never allow someone else to use your bank account.

VARIATIONS: Sweepstakes, lotteries, PayPal fraud, auction fraud, work at home frauds.

KEY WORDS: overpayment, third-party check, by accident, accidentally, wait until the check clears your bank, we will send you instructions where to wire the money, no risk, work at home, sweepstakes, lottery, government grant, scholarships.

COMMENT: You are legally responsible for checks and money orders that you deposit into your account. And there is no legitimate reason for anyone to give you a check and then ask you to return the money by wire.

PETS

THE SETUP: This wonderful dog, or exotic cat, or gorgeous bird, or fabulous horse needs a good home and unless we find one soon, the animal will be put down.

THE LIE: The photo of the animal in the ad was scanned in from some other website or a book of animal photos. The animal you're being asked to save doesn't exist, and no one is going to put it down.

THE SCAM: Playing off your sympathy and love of animals, you are asked to help save an animal by giving it a good home. What's more, it's yours for free.

WHAT'S REALLY HAPPENING: Whether the animal is going to be put down or the owners have fallen on hard times and simply can't keep it any longer, someone is going to give you a free dog, cat, bird, horse, whatever. They're doing it because this is best for the animal. The con men, who may claim to be missionaries, simply ask you to pay a small fee to transport the animal to you. So you pay the costs, but the animal doesn't arrive. Now the missionaries inform you that the poor animal has been impounded. Some will say by U.S. Customs, some will say by the ASPCA, and some will blame it on state or local animal rights' groups. Others will say that the animal couldn't be shipped on schedule because it's in sudden need of veterinary treatment. Unfortunately, you'll have to cover those costs, or this time the animal will be put down. It's hard to say no, but this is nothing more than a heartstring-pull advance fee fraud.

HOW TO PROTECT YOURSELF: Don't send money to people you don't know.

VARIATIONS: Similar to this are the scams that revolve around your own pet when it goes astray. You take out an ad in the paper, offering a reward, and someone calls to say he's found the animal. He may be a truck driver or traveling salesman who has taken the animal out of town with him, and wants a fee to return it. Or it may just be someone who says, I need to see the reward before I return the pet. And if you hesitate, he says, if you don't pay up now, I'll kill the animal. In most of those cases, the caller hasn't actually found your pet. It's just a scam.

KEY WORDS: needs a good home, will be put down, save this animal, stopped by U.S. Customs, impounded by the ASPCA, animal rights' groups.

COMMENT: This is a real minefield. Deal only with reputable agencies or don't get involved in saving animals.

HELP ME

THE SETUP: A desperate email (complete with grammar mistakes) arrives from someone you actually know:

> Please help me. I'm sorry I didn't inform you about my urgent trip to London, I don't have much time on the PC here, so I have to brief you my present situation which requires your urgent response actually, I had a trip to London but unfortunately for

me all my money got stolen at the hotel where I lodged due to a robbery incident that happened in the hotel. I had been so restless since last night because i have been without any money moreover the Hotel's telephone lines here got disconnected by the robbers and they are trying to get them fixed back I have access to only emails at the library because my mobile cant work here so I didnt bring it along, please I want you to help me with money so please can you send me 800 Pounds so when I return back I would refund it back to you as soon as I get home, I am so confused right now and dont know what to do, I had been to the embassy and they are currently looking into my case, Please you can send it through Western Union Money Transfer so I will get it immediately its sent, I want you to please help me transfer the money as soon as possible. Here is the details you need for the transfer below.

Receivers Names —
Receivers Address-
City- London
Country- UK
Zip Code- W1G 6AJ

Please get back to me as soon as you have the money sent, once you are done with the transfer just help me to scan a copy of the receipt given to you by Western Union or help me to write out the Money Transfer Control Number (MTCN).

THE LIE: The person you know who has written to you is not in London, doesn't need your help, and might not even know that his or her computer has been used to send this appeal to everyone in his or her address book.

THE SCAM: You think you're helping a friend in need. But the money is going straight to a Nigerian scammer.

WHAT'S REALLY HAPPENING: The scammer has infiltrated the victim's computer, putting a bug in there that has hijacked his address books — usually Outlook Express — and forced the computer to send the appeal for help to everyone on the list.

HOW TO PROTECT YOURSELF: The only thing you can do is to keep your anti-virus software up-to-date, and to install the latest fixes that will protect your system from malware attacks.

VARIATIONS: This is just another variation on the usual Western Union scam — wire the money but let me have the wiring instructions so I can get to Western Union and pick up the money before anyone can stop me.

KEY WORDS: Western Union, money transfer control number, please send me.

COMMENT: Payments through Western Union need to be considered very carefully.

PYRAMIDS

THE SETUP: You pay me for the right to join a club, and then you bring in new members and they pay you, and me, too, for the right to join a club, and those members bring in more members, and they pay all of us for the right to join a club. And we can all get rich.

THE LIE: The only person who's going to make money is the fellow at the top of the chain. All the rest will keep paying out to catch up until the pyramid collapses, which it will do.

THE SCAM: The profit is at the top, and the debt keeps getting passed lower. It's sometimes called franchise fraud because it hinges on your ability to franchise to new members and their right to franchise to new members.

WHAT'S REALLY HAPPENING: Pyramids are scams, no matter how they're disguised. Whether they're social networks, empowerment programs, religious gifting schemes, or investment clubs, because the numbers keep increasing geometrically, eventually it takes too many people to keep the pyramid going. It collapses and almost everyone loses money. That's why they're illegal.

HOW TO PROTECT YOURSELF: If a pyramid is pretending to be a multilevel marketing scheme, there has to be a product to sell, not simply the right to sell the right to sell. If you have to pay money for the right to hope you get it back from the people you bring into the scheme, it's a pyramid, and you're going to lose. Do not invest in franchises that require you to bring in new investors.

VARIATIONS: These schemes go by other

names: multilevel marketing, social networks, empowerment programs, religious
gifting schemes, women-only gifting
schemes, various franchise frauds, and many
investment clubs.

KEY WORDS: the right to join, bring in
new members, franchise fraud, multilevel
marketing, the right to sell the right to sell,
gifting, social networks, empowerment,
investment club.

COMMENT: Pyramids and chain letters
always collapse because their growth is not
sustainable.

SURVEYS

THE SETUP: You get the following email:

Congratulations! You've been selected to
take part in a quick and easy survey. In
return we will credit $50.00 to your ac-
count. This survey has only been sent to a
few people from our random generator.
Please spare a few minutes of your time
and take part in our online survey so we
at [fill in the blank with Walgreens, CVS
Pharmacies, Walmart, Rite-Aid, Dell Computers, Microsoft, Costco, Publix, Mc-

308

Donalds, or any recognizable company] can improve our services.

THE LIE: There is no survey, and none of the companies named has anything to do with this.

THE SCAM: The only thing you've been selected for is the theft of your identity.

WHAT'S REALLY HAPPENING: At the bottom of the invitation to take the survey is a link that you are supposed to copy and paste into your browser. As soon as you do, the malware hidden inside it goes to work to harvest your financial information, log-in codes, and password.

HOW TO PROTECT YOURSELF: Do not copy and paste anything into your browser, or click on links that have come through unsolicited emails.

VARIATIONS: If it's not a survey, it's a contest sponsored by the well-known company, a free gift for being a loyal customer, or a discount coupon for a future purchase.

KEY WORDS: congratulations, free survey, credit your account, coupon, discount, next purchase, loyal customer.

COMMENT: If you regularly do business with a company, they will address you by name. If you don't do business with them, don't expect them to give you something valuable just because it's Tuesday.

UNDERREPORTED INCOME
THE SETUP: An email (or letter) arrives from the IRS saying that you underreported your income for the previous year and are subject to both a review and possible criminal penalties.

THE LIE: The IRS doesn't send emails, and doesn't contact people out of the blue like that. If they have a problem, they will notify you by mail and discuss it with you face-to-face.

THE SCAM: The message looks very official, complete with a reference number that contains some part of your email address so that you can tell this isn't some mass-mailing fraud that goes out to several million people. It basically says: "Notice of Underreported Income — Please review your tax statement on Internal Revenue Service (IRS) website [with a link]."

WHAT'S REALLY HAPPENING: Hit the link and you will unknowingly download some malware that will ravage your files, looking for account information and passwords.

HOW TO PROTECT YOURSELF: Never hit links or do any downloads as a result of an unsolicited email, no matter who or what the email's origins claim to be.

VARIATIONS: Instead of unreported income, the typical variation is overpayment of tax and the promise of a refund.

KEY WORDS: underreported income, unreported income, tax evasion, refund, internal revenue, IRS, click on the link.

COMMENT: Do not open attachments. Do not reply. The following warning comes straight from the IRS: "The IRS does not initiate taxpayer communications through email. The IRS does not request detailed personal information through email. The IRS does not send email requesting your PIN numbers, passwords or similar access information for credit cards, banks or other financial accounts."

THE SETUP: A phone call comes in to a veteran — a man or a woman who has served in the U.S. military — claiming to be from the Department of Veterans Affairs.

THE LIE: The VA does not do this.

THE SCAM: The caller claims to be a VA worker who announces that the VA has changed its procedures on dispensing prescriptions and therefore needs to verify the veteran's credit card information.

WHAT'S REALLY HAPPENING: Identity theft.

HOW TO PROTECT YOURSELF: No matter who's calling, never divulge personal or financial information over the phone.

VARIATIONS: Calls from people claiming to be from government departments target veterans and military families to sell overpriced life insurance, to offer high-interest payday loans, to work car title and car repair scams, and to flog phony buyer discounts.

KEY WORDS: Department of Veterans Affairs, changed procedures, your credit card, dispensing prescriptions.

COMMENT: Report these calls to the Department of Veterans Affairs or your local police.

WIRING MONEY TO A TRUSTED THIRD PARTY

THE SETUP: You've found an ad for an apartment you think might be good for you, have spoken to the landlord, and set up an appointment to see it. But before you actually get to see the place, the landlord decides you're his kind of tenant and says, it's yours if you want it.

THE LIE: Whether there is an apartment for rent — or some product for sale — is immaterial. This is not about renting or buying anything, it's about convincing you to put up some money to show him how serious you are.

THE SCAM: You say that you want to see the apartment before you make any commitments, and he explains how that is very difficult for him. He says he's willing to take the apartment off the market and make the trip from someplace far away to show you that place, but he'll do it only if you're serious about renting it. You ask how could you possibly prove that, and he says, by paying the security deposit and one month's rent in advance. You tell him that's a nonstarter, and he tells you that he's willing to compromise. You don't have to pay him, you simply have to wire the money to a friend you trust who will promise to hold it for the landlord until you decide. He tells you pick a friend, any friend, and wire the money to him or her. Then, as soon as you send the receipt for the wire to the landlord, he'll make the arrangements to come to town to show you the apartment and hold it for you until you decide. If you don't want it, he assures you, your friend can simply send the money back to you. If you do want it, the friend can send the money to the landlord. Where's the catch? It's in the receipt. Once he's got it, he rushes to Western Union and picks up the money, using the correct wire information — which only the legitimate recipient should have — and a phony ID to claim that he's the friend you've named on the wire.

HOW TO PROTECT YOURSELF: Find another apartment that doesn't have such bizarre strings attached to it.

VARIATIONS: The same scam is used by people selling items long distance. Cars are often used, with the promise of shipping the car to you, but only after you wire money to your trusted friend.

KEY WORDS: Western Union, your friend, money in advance.

COMMENT: Do not wire money to anyone as part of any deal with someone you do not know. If a deal has too many odd strings attached to it, be very suspicious.

WORK AT HOME

THE SETUP: You can earn money in the comfort of your own home, even while watching television. Perfect for the elderly, young mothers, and students.

THE LIE: The only company that's going to make any money here is the one supposedly hiring you to stuff envelopes.

THE SCAM: The ads in newspapers, magazines, or on the Internet promise you that you can earn money from home by doing simple tasks. "No telephone to answer, no selling, no customers to deal with." In this instance, the simple task is stuffing envelopes. Various companies, the ads claim, will pay you, say, 25¢ to put their brochures and sales letters in preaddressed envelopes. Do a thousand a day, and you can pick up $250. If that's not enough, some of these ads boast, "Potential earnings up to $250,000 per year." These are proven opportunities that come with full online support via email. It's a win-win situation. The companies save tens of thousands of dollars by hiring you to work at home, and you earn all this money for doing very little. Just send away for the starter kit, and you can be earning thousands before the end of the week.

WHAT'S REALLY HAPPENING: A perfect way for the elderly, young mothers, and students to get ripped off, this is a variation of an advance fee pyramid that will cost you more than you earn. The starter kit will require you to do two very important things before you can earn anything. First, you will have to sign on to the program to become an associate of the company offering you the work from home deal. After all, the company will explain, our reputation is such that we can't have just anybody stuffing envelopes for us because we need to protect our good name.

So to become an associate, you have to fill out a form and enclose the associate's fee of, say, $100. That might stop some people, but here's the guarantee. If the company doesn't accept you as an associate, your money will be returned. So there's no risk. Needless to say, no one is refused, which means there's no need to return any of these advance fees. Now comes the second part of the deal. You will be required to place ads in your local newspaper which read, word for word, like the one you've just responded to. In other words, your ads will bring in new associates. That might stop some people, because it's going to cost them another, say, $50 to $100 to buy the ads. Except you're already in for $100, and anyway, the company is going to pay you to do this, so you can recoup those fees. The sample ads they provide contain your name and address. The ad says that each response must be accompanied with a first-class stamp and, say, a quarter to cover mailing costs. You get to keep all the quarters simply for stuffing the respondents' information into an envelope and sending it on to the company. They in turn contact the respondents and try to seduce them into becoming associates and buying more ads. It is true that you can earn up to two hundred and fifty grand a year. But in order to do that, at 25¢ per response from the ads you've paid for, you'll need to stuff a million envelopes.

HOW TO PROTECT YOURSELF: There are plenty of ways to earn money while working from home. But none of the legitimate ones requires you to pay someone an up-front fee for the privilege.

VARIATIONS: It's the same scam when you see ads that read, "Earn money while taking online Internet surveys," "Earn at home while reading books," and "Become a mystery shopper." They're all pyramid scams that will require you pay up front for the privilege of bringing in new victims, or scams in which overpayments will be made. Also included here are surveys and other "work at home" scams.

KEY WORDS: work at home, earn at home, make money from home, make money online, no selling, high potential, proven opportunity, no risk, stuff envelopes, mystery shopper, surveys, steady income, minimal work, we will pay you.

COMMENT: When someone offers you an

opportunity to make money but insists you have to pay for the opportunity up front, you're being ripped off. Do not send money to strangers on the promise that you will somehow receive more money back from them.

PART THREE

CHAPTER FOURTEEN:
THE 39 STEPS

WHAT YOU NEED TO DO TO PROTECT YOURSELF FROM FRAUD

Common sense is the single most important ingredient in protecting yourself, your family, or your business against fraud because common sense is what the con man is hoping you don't have.

For a fraudster to succeed, he has to be smooth enough to convince you to hand him your money, even when that funny feeling in the pit of your stomach keeps nagging — something about this isn't quite right.

Life isn't always about going with your gut instincts, but staying safe from fraud is about giving yourself time to think about what your instincts are telling you.

What follows is a checklist of ways that will help you keep alert to frauds, even those that haven't been profiled in the previous chapters. You may read through them and say, this is only common sense and I know that already. But common sense isn't always on the job. The con men are looking for those whose guards are down. And they're very clever at disguising their true intentions as they feed on your gullibility or naiveté.

1. Keep in mind that fraud is a two-way street crime, which means that before a con man can do any harm, you have to open the door. To get you to let him in, a fraudster will employ every trick he can think of and all the chicanery he can muster. Therefore, never allow yourself to be rushed into a decision. Always take the time to step away, to get some perspective, and to think about what's happening. Just a few extra minutes can be enough to protect you from a great deal of harm.

2. Fraudsters will always take the course of least resistance. If you make life too difficult for them, they will seek greener pastures. So before revealing personal information to anyone you don't know, ask yourself, would I tell this to a stranger on the street?

3. Whenever you are contacted by someone you don't know — whether it's by phone, snail mail, email, or in person — and the person offers you something that, on the surface, sounds attractive, you must look below the surface. Ask yourself, what's in

it for him? And ask yourself, what will it cost me if everything goes wrong? Always think *downside.*

4. If the person who invites you into a deal is someone you know and especially some- one who, perhaps, you think of as a friend, that's no guarantee that the deal is good or that the person is honest.

5. Keep an eye open for anomalies. Look for variations from predictable behavior. Look for things that seem out of place. Listen for things that don't sound right. If you see it or hear it, ask yourself, why?

6. No matter what someone says to you, or how much you want to believe it, there is no such thing as an investment without risk or a guarantee that you cannot lose.

7. Before you do any business with anybody — whether you are buying, investing, or becoming someone's partner in a money- making scheme — it is essential that you find out who he is and what his business is all about. Google, Bing, and dozens of online search engines can reveal a multi- tude of sins. Check names, addresses, phone numbers, backgrounds, and key words. (See the Key Word Index on page 345.) Reliable companies and legitimate offers can be substantiated through a good search or by contacting reputable services

such as the Better Business Bureau. Con artists and scams cannot stand up to serious scrutiny, and the deeper you go online, the more they will show up as con artists and scams.

8. Take precautions when buying and selling online. If you're buying, check the seller's references. If you're selling, make sure that the payment has actually cleared your bank before you send the item to the buyer.

9. If you're not 100% sure that what you're buying is real, it's best not to buy. If you're not 100% sure that the other party is honest, it's best not to deal with that other party. Short of that, if you do buy or sell when you still have doubts, insist on using an online escrow service. And do not automatically assume that the escrow service recommended by the other party is legit. Con men have set up sites that pretend to be an escrow service as a tool for committing fraud. Check out as many escrow services as possible, and only settle on one that you are 100% comfortable with. eBay's recommendation is Escrow .com (www.escrow.com).

10. Do not pay money to receive money. Wiring a stranger a fee on the promise of receiving a big prize, to obtain a service,

to reduce or consolidate debt, or to remedy a bad credit rating is utter foolishness. The most common scams right now involve asking consumers to wire money in order to get a larger amount in return. It won't work.

11. Paying by credit card is better than paying by check. Paying by wire or money order is not a good idea, especially if the person you're paying insists that you wire or money order the payment to him. The reason why is obvious. Your credit card offers a level of protection that checks, cash, and wires don't. If something goes wrong, your credit card company will stand behind you, at least for a little while.

12. If your card goes missing, report it immediately.

13. When paying with a credit card or using your card at an ATM, always take your receipts. If you don't save them, then shred them. It's astonishing how many receipts are left at ATMs and gas pumps.

14. Never leave your card with anyone, such as a hotel front desk, a restaurant waiter, or shop. Always insist that your card be swiped in front of you. Most restaurants will process your card at a cash desk — often out of your sight — so be cautious when doing business in a place you don't

know. Double swiping, using a second card reader out of sight, is how your card gets cloned. And it happens more frequently than most people suspect in restaurants, bars, and shops.

15. If you pay your credit card bill by check, don't put the entire card number on the check. Use only the last four digits.

16. Regularly check your credit reports. You are entitled to free copies every year (www.annualcreditreport.com) and you need to see them.

17. If you suspect something isn't right about your credit report, contact the agency. You are entitled to correct any incorrect information.

18. If you suspect someone has stolen your identity, or is trying to, contact the credit reporting agencies and ask them to add fraud alerts to your file. That's a red flag to banks and financial institutions that someone is trying to do you harm.

19. Verify bank and credit card statements carefully. Because they arrive regularly, you should know when a statement is missing. Notify your bank or credit card company right away. And immediately report any charges that shouldn't be there.

20. If two or more statements don't arrive, contact the post office to see if someone

has deliberately changed your address. Then contact all of your credit card companies, utility companies, and banks to see if your address has been changed there. If that's happened, file a charge right away with the post office authorities, then notify everyone you do business with — again, credit card companies, utilities, banks, and credit reporting services — that there is a problem.

21. If you are going to provide someone with your card number, either by phone or online, be absolutely certain that they are reliable. Consider the fact that anyone obtaining your credit card number, the card expiration date, and three-digit ID that appears on the back can then use that card to buy something online or over the phone. Card not present fraud is rampant. So be very careful to whom you hand that key to your credit card.

22. There is no reason whatsoever to provide your Social Security number to anyone, at any point, during a credit card transaction. There is no requirement to do so. Nor should you.

23. If a telemarketer phones, before you tell him anything about yourself, find out as much as you can about him. Remember, he's not your friend, he's a salesman. Ask

his name, address, and phone number. Ask about his company, who they are, and where they are. Some con artists give out false names, telephone numbers, addresses, and business license numbers. You can verify the accuracy of what he says by explaining that you need to phone back. You can check unfamiliar companies with your local consumer protection agency, Better Business Bureau, state attorney general, the National Fraud Information Center, or other watchdog groups. Legitimate companies will also give you whatever details you need to establish that they are legitimate. By contrast, con men will do as much double-talk as necessary to keep you on the line.

24. If you are interested in what's being sold, ask that written information be sent to you by mail. Legitimate companies will do it. Con men will try to talk you out of it. Even then beware because not everything that's written down is true.

25. When your gut tells you something is wrong, err on the side of caution.

26. Don't believe testimonials. For a fee, celebrities will sell anything.

27. Beware of sellers who say, "You must act now or the offer won't be good"; "You've won a free prize but, of course,

you will have to pay postage, handling, and insurance"; "No need to check the company, we've been around twenty-five years and never had a complaint." Never commit yourself to paying for anything unless you've got it in writing, are 100% sure what you're paying for now, that you want it, and how much it will cost you later.

28. Get the return agreement in writing. It should spell out what happens if you don't want it, if the goods or service aren't what the salesman promised they would be, or if whatever you've purchased turns out not to work.

29. Before you send money to anyone, ask yourself, "What guarantees do I have?" Conditions need to be spelled out clearly, and they need to be enforceable.

30. If you are making a major purchase, or committing yourself to a serious amount of money, always consult an attorney before you sign anything.

31. Protect all your computers. There are loads of good antivirus programs and spam filters that can sort out malware, suspect downloads, and scam emails. Find one you like and keep it up-to-date. Mailwasher (www.mailwasher.net) bounces spam back to the sender marked "undeliv-

erable." The idea is that spammers will see no one lives at that address and take your name off their mailing lists. While that may be a bit of wishful thinking, at least Mailwasher does inspect your emails while they're still on the server, instead of already downloaded. Two software programs that have become indispensable are Spybot and AdAware. Spybot (www.safer-networking.org) searches for spyware and gets rid of it. AdAware (www.lavasoft.com) is an adware and spy removal tool. Best of all, there are free editions of both. Also, every computer needs a firewall, up-to-date antivirus programs, and a pop-up blocker.

32. Never open an attachment or download anything that comes in an email from someone you don't know, or don't totally trust. Violating this rule is the surest way to become a victim of identity theft.

33. Refrain from the temptation of using passwords and PINs that are obvious. If someone tries to guess your passwords and PINs, he'll start with names, birth dates, phone numbers, and addresses. It's best to use a combination of seemingly random letters and numbers. Then, never reveal your passwords or PINs to anyone. Your personal information needs to stay

personal. The more people who know it, the more chance there is for abuse. If someone asks for your Social Security number, bank account information, credit card information, and so on, demand to know why. Legitimate banks, credit card companies, and websites will never contact you to ask for that information.

34. While you should always keep a list of important numbers — credit card numbers and bank account numbers — they should be stored in a secure place. If you also write down your passwords and PINs, they should be separated, hidden in different places, and definitely not in the same place as your credit card and bank account numbers.

35. Change your passwords and PINs often enough that they will be impossible to crack.

36. When the time comes to buy a new computer, make sure you fully erase the hard drive of your old computer, using a program that overwrites everything several times. You need to make it nearly impossible for anyone to find out what used to be there. If you are throwing out the computer, remove the hard drive and destroy it.

37. If you run a business, institute a clean

desk policy. Sensitive information and anything that might be of value to an identity thief needs to be locked away at the close of business. People do get into offices at night, including cleaning crews, so nothing of value should be available to them.

38. Buy a shredder and use it when you throw out letters, bills, statements, correspondence, old credit cards, or, in fact, anything that contains personal information. Also, shred old computer backup CDs and DVDs.

39. Never forget that what you do online stays online.

RESOURCES

A List of Important Addresses and Numbers

The Credit Reporting Agencies

All three major agencies will help you should you fall victim to identity theft. You should notify all three and then ask for a copy of your credit report. In fact, it's a good idea to ask for a free copy every year from all three agencies. It's not only good to know who's got information on you and to see for yourself what they've got, it's also good to know who's been asking about your credit status.

You are entitled to a free credit report every year, and can obtain it by logging on to www.annualcreditreport.com. That site has links to the three main reporting agencies, which can otherwise be found here:

Equifax
Fraud Alert System

P.O. Box 105496
Atlanta, GA 30348-5496
800-525-6285
www.equifax.com

Experian
Customer Service
P.O. Box 2104
Allen, TX 75013-2104
888-397-3742
www.experian.com

Trans Union
Fraud Victim Assistance Department
P.O. Box 390
Springfield, PA 19064-0390
800-680-7289
www.transunion.com

Places to Turn to for Help

The **Federal Trade Commission** (FTC) is the lead government agency in protecting consumers from fraud. Although the FTC does not resolve individual consumer problems, the commission does initiate some investigations into various types of fraud, including identity theft and scam emails. How to file a complaint with the FTC is explained at www.ftc.gov/bcp/edu/micro sites/idtheft/consumers/filing-a-report.html.

They also have a complaint assistance wizard at www.ftccomplaintassistant.gov. Unsolicited spam and phishing emails should be forwarded to them at spam@uce.gov. The FTC Identity Theft Hotline is 877-ID-THEFT (877-438-4338; TTY: 866-653-4261).

The **National Do Not Call Registry** on-line registration form can be found at www.donotcall.gov/register/reg.aspx or by phone, 888-382-1222 (TTY: 866-290-4236).

Similarly, the **Direct Marketing Association** runs two do not contact lists. The first is for direct mail. The second is for email. Although it must be said that results of the do not email list are sporadic. You can register for one or both at www.dma choice.org/dma/member/regist.action. Otherwise, you can send complaints to:

The Federal Trade Commission
Consumer Response Center
600 Pennsylvania Avenue NW
Washington, DC 20580

The **Social Security Administration** (SSA) also maintains a fraud hotline at 800-269-0271 (TTY: 866-501-2101; fax: 410-597-0118). Fraud can be reported to the

SSA at www.socialsecurity.gov/oig/public_
fraud_reporting/form.htm. Otherwise, their
address is:

Social Security Fraud Hotline
P.O. Box 17768
Baltimore, MD 21235

The **Internet Crime Complaint Center**
(IC3) offers, perhaps, the most convenient
way to file an Internet-related fraud complaint (www.ic3.gov). A joint venture of the
FBI (www.fbi.gov), the National White Collar Crime Center (www.nw3c.org), and the
Bureau of Justice Assistance (www.ojp.usdoj
.gov/bja), the IC3 offers a simple and
straightforward Complaint Referral Form at
www.ic3.gov/complaint/default.aspx. After
evaluating a complaint, the IC3 may then
refer it to a federal, state, local, or international law enforcement agency or a regula-
tory body.
Further information is available from:

The National White Collar Crime Center
10900 Nuckols Road, Suite 325
Glen Allen, VA 23060

The **Internal Revenue Service** (IRS)
publishes online advice called Tax Fraud

Alerts (www.irs.gov/compliance/enforce ment). They also offer very good advice on phishing and identity theft scams at www .irs.gov/privacy/article/0,,id=179820,00 .html. If you receive a phishing email, they ask that you forward it to phishing@irs.gov.

The **Federal Bureau of Investigation** (FBI) operates a dedicated cybercrime unit, which is best contacted through your local field office. Addresses and phone numbers can be found in the phone book or at www.fbi.gov/contact/fo/fo.htm.

The **Secret Service** also investigates fraud, and for years maintained a database of Nigerian 419 scams. Unfortunately, the database became too unwieldily and expensive to maintain. However, they still have a serious interest in advance fee schemes and frauds that involve monetary instruments, such as counterfeit bonds, negotiable paper, and currency. Contact should be through a local field office. Check the phone book or www.secretservice.gov/field_offices.shtml.

The **U.S. Postal Service** investigates fraud when it involves the misuse of the U.S. mail system. Their home page is https:// postalinspectors.uspis.gov. Mail fraud schemes are explained at https://postal inspectors.uspis.gov/investigations/Mail Fraud/fraudschemes/FraudSchemes.aspx. If you want to report mail fraud, you can do that online at https://postalinspectors.uspis.gov/forms/MailFraudComplaint.aspx. They also have an online form to report identity theft at https://postalinspectors.uspis.gov/forms/IDTheft.aspx. Their fraud hotline is 877-876-2455. Complaints can also be sent by mail to:

Inspection Service Support Group
222 South Riverside Plaza, Suite 1250
Chicago, IL 60606

The **National Consumers League** is a private, nonprofit advocacy group that runs two important websites, www.fraud.org and www.phishinginfo.org. The NCL also provides an online fraud complaint form, which, they say, they pass along to law enforcement (https://secure.nclforms.org/nficweb/nfic.htm). Call 202-835-3323 or fax 202-835-0747. For snail mail:

National Consumers League
1701 K Street NW, Suite 1200
Washington, DC 20006

The **Better Business Bureau** is not government-run but rather a licensed charity whose mission is to help consumers find legitimate and trusted businesses. Their home page (www.bbb.org) will ask for a ZIP code so that you can go directly to the BBB nearest you or it will allow you to go to the U.S. or Canadian site.

ACKNOWLEDGMENTS

Having written about fraud for many years, I have literally hundreds of people who need to be thanked for giving me an education in the black art of chicanery. I hope they will accept my thanks as a group. That said, most are part of larger organizations that include the U.S. Department of Justice, the FBI, ICE in its present form and as U.S. Customs in its previous life, the U.S. Secret Service, the U.S. Postal Inspectors Service, the U.S. Department of the Treasury, the Internal Revenue Service, the Internet Crimes Complaint Center, the Social Security Administration, the U.S. Federal Trade Commission, the National White Collar Crime Center, Equifax, Experian, Trans Union, the Office of the District Attorney of Manhattan, the Office of the U.S. Attorney for the Southern District of New York, the Office of the U.S. Attorney for the Eastern District of New York, and my old pals at the Economic Crime Department of the City of London Police, in Great Britain.

I am also grateful to my friends at *Barron's* magazine, to the wonderful Mel Berger and his terrific assistant Graham Jaenicke, and to John Duff at Perigee who gets my vote for the best in the business.

And, *comme d'habitude,* La Benayoun.

KEY WORD INDEX

The following list represents key words that you are likely to read or hear in a fraudster's pitch. The second part of the entry refers to the relevant scam or scams discussed in Part Two.

345

assist to purchase this product: *agent for hire*

avoid double claiming: *lottery*

bank draft: *FedEx*

become a partner: *inheritance fraud*

bill collectors: *debt management*

black currency: *black money*

bring in new members: *pyramid*

buy your home: *home foreclosure*

by accident: *overpayment*

call back: *area code 809*

call immediately: *area code 809, missed phone call*

call this number: *missed phone call*

Canadian National Lottery: *lottery*

cancel your late fees: *debt management*

cannot quote its content: *FedEx*

can't fail: *hot stock tips*

changed procedures: *veterans hoax*

check as a deposit: *check fraud*

clean the bills: *black money*

click on the link: *credit card, IRS refund, underreported income*

computer ballot system: *lottery*

computer generated: *lottery*

computer sweepstakes: *lottery*

conduct surveys: *work at home*

confidential: *agent for hire*

confirm your password: *credit card*

confirmation of address/utility services:

gold dust

congratulations: *lottery, survey*

consolidating debt: *debt management*

contact our agent: *lottery*

contact our delivery department: *FedEx*

coupon: *survey*

courier shipment number: *auction parcel fraud*

credit agencies: *debt management*

credit card: *veterans hoax*

credit history: *low-interest guaranteed loan*

credit your account: *survey*

dear prize winner: *lottery*

debt counseling: *debt management*

deed your home: *home foreclosure*

Department of Veterans Affairs: *veterans hoax*

DHL: *auction parcel fraud, FedEx*

did not need to buy a ticket: *lottery*

did not need to enter: *lottery*

discount: *survey*

dispensing prescriptions: *veterans hoax*

do not let anyone deceive you: *FedEx*

earn at home: *work at home*

earn money while shopping: *mystery shopper*

economic stimulus: *IRS refund*

eligible to receive a tax refund: *IRS refund*

eliminate your bank overdraft: *debt elimination*
eliminate your credit card debts: *debt elimination*
eliminate your mortgage: *debt elimination*
empowerment: *pyramid*
exempt organizations: *IRS refund*
expired: *credit card*
export fees: *gold dust*
failure to appear: *jury duty*
FedEx: *auction parcel fraud, FedEx*
final winning notification: *lottery*
fiscal activity: *IRS refund*
foolproof: *multilevel marketing*
for your protection: *escrow fraud*
foreclosure: *debt management*
franchise fraud: *pyramid*
free: *survey*
funds transfer number: *auction parcel fraud*
get in now: *hot stock tips*
gifting: *pyramid*
global software promotions: *lottery*
going bankrupt: *debt management*
government grant: *overpayment*
group of like-minded victims: *loss recovery*
guarantee everything is in order: *auction parcel fraud*
guaranteed: *low-interest guaranteed loan*
harassment: *debt management*
high potential: *work at home*

I've used them before: *escrow fraud*
impounded by the ASPCA: *pet fraud*
in order to collect: *lottery*
inherit: *inheritance fraud*
inspect our product: *gold dust*
instructions where to wire the money:
    overpayment
insurance fee: *low-interest guaranteed loan*
interest payments: *debt management*
into your bank account: *inheritance fraud*
investment and procurement: *agent for hire*
investment club: *pyramid*
IRS: *IRS form W-9095, IRS refund, under-*
    reported income
IRS Antifraud Commission: *IRS refund*
IRS tax form: *IRS form W-9095*
issues bonds and promissory notes: *debt*
    elimination
kill you: *hitman/killer for hire*
land patent: *home foreclosure fraud II*
leave the payee blank and I'll fill it in later:
    check fraud
legally satisfies all of your debts: *debt elimi-*
    nation
lottery: *area code 809, overpayment*
love to shop: *mystery shopper*
low interest: *low-interest guaranteed loan*
lower your interest rates: *debt management*
loyal customer: *survey*
lump-sum payout: *lottery*

make money from home: *work at home*

make money online: *work at home*

minimal work: *work at home*

missed call: *missed phone call*

MoneyGram: *auction parcel fraud*

money in advance: *wiring money to a trusted third party*

money transfer control number: *please help me, Western Union*

multilevel marketing: *pyramid*

must go up: *hot stock tips*

mystery shopper: *work at home*

necessary payment procedure: *FedEx*

needs a good home: *pet fraud*

next purchase: *survey*

Nigeria: *FedEx, overpayment*

no risk: *overpayment*

no selling: *work at home*

no time to waste: *hot stock tips*

non-circumvention: *agent for hire*

non-disclosure: *agent for hire*

online customer satisfaction survey: *IRS refund*

our only contact: *agent for hire*

our security protocol: *lottery*

overpaid taxes: *IRS refund*

pay me: *hitman/killer for hire*

pay off your mortgage: *home foreclosure*

pay us enabling money: *gold dust*

pay you one-third: *inheritance fraud*

pay your costs: *home foreclosure*
paying off your debts: *debt management*
perfectly legal: *debt elimination*
personal or business use: *low-interest guaranteed loan*
power of attorney: *debt elimination*
prize: *area code 809*
processing fee: *low-interest guaranteed loan*
promotional: *lottery*
prove your identity: *jury duty*
proven opportunity: *work at home*
registered with us for shipping: *FedEx*
relative: *area code 809*
repair your credit rating: *home foreclosure*
required by the IRS: *IRS form W-9095*
rescue package: *home foreclosure*
return the call: *area code 809*
the right to join: *pyramid*
the right to sell the right to sell: *pyramid*
routine maintenance: *credit card*
satisfied with our product: *gold dust*
save this animal: *pet fraud*
scan copy of your passport or driver's license: *gold dust*
scholarships: *overpayment*
secret shopper: *mystery shopper*
security code: *credit card II*
seize the assets: *loss recovery*
selling the right to sell the right: *multilevel marketing*

share the expenses: *loss recovery*

sign the check and we'll print it in the register: *check fraud*

smuggled: *black money*

social networks: *pyramid*

someone you trust: *wiring money to a trusted third party*

sovereign territory: *home foreclosure fraud II*

special chemical: *black money*

special detergent: *black money*

special ink: *black money*

special liquid: *black money*

steady income: *work at home*

stolen: *credit card*

stopped by U.S. Customs: *pet fraud*

store it securely until payment: *auction parcel fraud*

submit the tax refund request: *IRS refund*

surveys: *work at home*

suspended: *credit card*

suspicious charges: *credit card*

sweepstakes: *overpayment*

take over: *hot stock tips*

tax avoidance investigation: *IRS refund*

tax evasion: *IRS, underreported income*

tax refund: *IRS refund*

taxpayer identification number: *IRS form W-9095*

third-party check: *overpayment*
third-party guarantee: *auction parcel fraud*
three-digit PIN: *credit card II*
trial shipment: *gold dust*
unclaimed: *inheritance fraud*
unresolved tax problems: *IRS refund*
unusual pattern of activity: *credit card II*
UPS: *auction parcel fraud, FedEx*
urgent: *area code 809*
U.S. Post Office: *auction parcel fraud, FedEx*
usual purchases: *credit card II*
valued customer: *FedEx*
very good escrow service: *escrow fraud*
W-8888: *IRS form W-9095*
W-88BEN: *IRS form W-9095*
W-9095: *IRS form W-9095*
wait until the check clears: *overpayment*
want you dead: *hitman/killer for hire*
warrant for your arrest: *jury duty*
we will pay you: *work at home*
we wish to come to your country: *agent for hire*
West Africa: *FedEx*
Western Union: *auction parcel fraud, please help me, wiring money to a trusted third party*
white money: *black money*
will be put down: *pet fraud*
you will have to pay the sum of: *FedEx*

your account: *area code 809*
your commission: *agent for hire*
your friend: *wiring money to a trusted third party*

INDEX

scams *(Continued)*

ABOUT THE AUTHOR

Jeffrey Robinson, journalist and author of more than twenty-five books, is an internationally recognized expert on organized crime, fraud, and money laundering. Named "the world's most important financial crime journalist" by the British Bankers' Association, he was based in London, England, for more than twenty-five years and now lives in New York.